WHAT'S WRONG WITH MINDFULNESS
(AND WHAT ISN'T)

WHAT'S WRONG

with **MINDFULNESS**

(AND WHAT ISN'T)

Zen Perspectives

Edited by
Robert Meikyo Rosenbaum
and Barry Magid

Wisdom

Wisdom Publications, Inc.
199 Elm Street
Somerville, MA 02144 USA
wisdompubs.org

Library of Congress Cataloging-in-Publication Data
Names: Rosenbaum, Robert, editor. Magid, Barry, editor.
Title: What's wrong with mindfulness (and what isn't) : Zen perspectives /
    edited by Robert Meikyo Rosenbaum and Barry Magid.
Description: Somerville : Wisdom Publications, 2016. | Includes
    bibliographical references and index.
Identifiers: LCCN 2016000557| ISBN 9781614292838 (pbk. : alk. paper) | ISBN
    1614292833 (pbk. : alk. paper)
Subjects: LCSH: Meditation—Buddhism. | Zen Buddhism—Doctrines.
Classification: LCC BQ5612 .W48 2016 | DDC 294.3/442—dc23
LC record available at https://lccn.loc.gov/2016000557

ISBN 978-1-61429-283-8   ebook ISBN 978-1-61429-307-1

20 19 18 17 16   5 4 3 2 1

Cover design by Philip Pascuzzo. Interior design by Jordan Wannemacher.
Set in Minion Pro 10.25 pt. /15 pt.

Norman Fischer's poem "Solitude" was previously published in James Year's online magazine *Across the Margin.*

"When Mindfulness Is Too Much" and the dialogue between Gil Fronsdal and Max Erdstein was originally published in *Inquiring Mind* 31, no. 2 (Spring 2015). © 2015 by *Inquiring Mind.* inquiringmind.com. It is reprinted by permission of *Inquiring Mind.*

The epilogue is reproduced by permission of SAGE Publications Ltd., London, Los Angeles, New Delhi, Singapore, and Washington, DC, from Robert H. Sharf, "Is Mindfulness Buddhist? (And Why It Matters)," *Transcultural Psychiatry,* Copyright © Robert H. Sharf, 2014.

Wisdom Publications' books are printed on acid-free paper and meet the guidelines for permanence and durability of the Production Guidelines for Book Longevity of the Council on Library Resources.

🌸 This book was produced with environmental mindfulness. For more information, please visit wisdompubs.org/wisdom-environment.

Printed in the United States of America.

MIX
Paper from
responsible sources
FSC
www.fsc.org   FSC® C011935

Please visit fscus.org.

TABLE OF CONTENTS

INTRODUCTION

UNIVERSAL MINDFULNESS—
BE CAREFUL WHAT YOU WISH FOR?

Robert Meikyo Rosenbaum
and Barry Magid

ZEN TEACHERS SPEAK TO MINDFULNESS

Half a century ago, Zen was the magic elixir that would save all of us in the West from ourselves. Beat poetry, the inner game of tennis, and the art of motorcycle maintenance—even the nostrums of business management manuals all claimed to bear Zen's imprimatur. Zen, with its spare aesthetic and paradoxical stories, seemed to offer an antidote to the stresses of conformity and the false promises of commercialism. As a bonus, it apparently provided a tried and true pathway to enlightenment for the spiritual seeker.

With time we learned that Zen is—as it likes to proclaim—nothing special. Its practitioners are not exempted from ordinary human frailties. Throughout its history in Asia, Zen, far from being the rarefied panacea we had imagined, suffered its disappointments and its scandals, its organizational struggles, personal rivalries, and internecine doctrinal conflicts. Zen in America and Europe also turned out to not be immune from muddles and missteps. This was disillusioning but also, ultimately, refreshing: rather than pretending to be some precious, idealized practice, Zen in the West had to become real.

Being real means engaging with all the bits and pieces of everyday life. But what should that look like? A series of woodblock prints famous in the Zen tradition—the Ox-Herding Pictures—depicts the various stages of a spiritual journey. The tenth and final picture depicts the culmination of practice as "returning to the marketplace with bliss-bestowing hands." The marketplace represents the hubbub of daily life with its jostle and noise, its glitter and its dust; this tenth Ox-Herding picture offers a vision of how a mature practitioner, forged by the rigors of the long quest, is able to return to everyday affairs and be "in the world but not of it." Appearing as deeply ordinary, still she lives a life that supports the liberation of all beings.

In Zen we like to say "the lotus blooms in the mud... and the mud is pretty interesting, too." Since its arrival in the West, Zen has had its share of mud: teachers who did not live up to the ethical standards expected of them; difficulties supporting some practice centers while other groups thrived using commercial business models; arguments about how to stay true to tradition while also fostering the emergence of new forms of practice. In spite of and sometimes even because of these difficulties, Zen in the West has provided a deeply satisfying spiritual path for many, and the liberation it offers not only survived its journey to the West but has arguably been reinvigorated as its devoted practitioners struggled to make sense of it in its new time and place.

Now it is mindfulness's turn to be appropriated by Western culture as the philosopher's stone. Sometimes idealized as a cure-all and sometimes vilified as a New Age pablum, it has spread into society at large and, like Zen, expanded beyond its original training venues, religious practices, and cultural contexts. "Mindfulness" is becoming a generic term whose meaning becomes less clear in direct proportion to the hype it generates. It can be found everywhere; corporate retreats, medical centers, sports facilities, and even the military have adopted it as a way to decrease stress and improve performance.

Mindfulness has indeed entered the marketplace in the West, but it is questionable whether its hands are always bliss bestowing; there is even a danger of them becoming as grasping as all the other hands to be found there. This is not because mindfulness's proponents are greedily chasing after money—though sadly that seems to be a not-infrequent phenomenon—but because the movement seems preoccupied with results. This goal-oriented grasping has streamlined and mass marketed what Chögyam Trungpa Rinpoche, a generation ago, so aptly called "spiritual materialism."

The Heart Sutra, a text at the very core of Mahayana Buddhist teaching, proclaims there is "no path, no wisdom, and no gain." "No gain" is the very antithesis of spiritual materialism; it rejects any means-to-an-end conceptualization or use of meditation. Preserving the centrality of "no gain" is how Zen can potentially maintain its integrity in the midst of a marketplace-based society. To the extent that it has been able to do so, Zen, for all its stumbles and excesses, is uniquely positioned to serve as an exemplar to the mindfulness movement as it makes its own attempt to bring a Buddhist practice to the world without the world in turn contaminating the heart of Buddhist practice.

The Zen teachers assembled here, representing many different lineages and styles of teaching, have all been deeply schooled in the attitude of "no gain." We also have practical experience wrestling with the knotty issue of how to take practices derived from Asian Buddhism and adapt them to our Western context while remaining true to the healthy roots on which they rely. For instance, all of us are engaged in teaching laypeople who may never see the inside of a monastery and who certainly will not live lives adhering to the strict list of precepts that govern Buddhist monastics. Although mindfulness is most intimately associated with the Theravada or Vipassana traditions, mindfulness also plays an important role in Zen (though often in subtly different forms). We hope by sharing our perspectives we may be able to contribute some insight to the issues our friends in the mindfulness movement face.

LOST IN TRANSLATION?

Zen in America has itself been subject to three powerfully destabilizing trends: secularization (taking practice out of its monastic context with its associated religious rituals), instrumentalization (for example, using meditation as a "technique" for realizing personal self-transformation), and deracination (extracting Buddhist practices from their cultural and historical roots). All of the authors in this book are concerned, though, that the mindfulness movement sometimes carries these trends to extremes. Removed from its rich—and rigorously ascetic—Theravadin Buddhist context, mindfulness has been imported to the West as a fully secularized technique that can be learned and practiced over the course of a few weeks or even within the confines of a weekend workshop. This consumer-oriented, quick-fix approach to meditation, which has come to be dubbed "McMindfulness," has raised serious questions in our minds about the trends of which we are a part.

Traditionally Buddhist teachings were conveyed face to face and mind to mind, requiring a close relationship between student and teacher, along with the intimacy that arises when people live together, in the day-to-day activities of a community. A poem frequently recited in Zen Buddhist temples starts off "The mind of the great sage of India is conveyed intimately from west to east." According to tradition, Zen began when Buddha taught an assembly of followers by simply holding up a flower; his disciple Mahakashyapa smiled, and Buddha declared the transmission was complete. This intimacy was and, we feel, continues to be crucial—and in stark contrast to some of the ways mindfulness is taught today, when it is presented didactically in classrooms or as sound bites in seminars.

Many teachers of mindfulness work hard to ensure Buddhist teachings are transmitted intimately and thoroughly in their new contexts. Jack Kornfield, Joseph Goldstein, and Sharon Salzberg, for instance, have retained the major elements of Buddhist psychology and phenomenology in the creation of Insight Meditation. Others, like Jon Kabat-Zinn, have separated the techniques of awareness from their Buddhist roots so as to create therapeutic techniques that can be focused on stress reduction and other medical uses. We applaud the sincere thoughtfulness of this approach and how the Center for Mindfulness has labored to specify training requirements for its teachers, but we wonder if even a well-designed training regimen can develop, in a year or two, the kind of spiritual depth Zen Buddhist training develops over what is usually decades of rigorous practice (or, for that matter, the kind of psychological acumen therapists usually need many years of training to acquire).

Further afield, we are concerned when mindfulness morphs into myriad strains of self-improvement, self-actualization, and sometimes, it seems, simply the self-involvement of a consumerist culture.

Around 1227 CE, Eihei Dogen, the founder of Soto Zen in Japan, wrote an introduction to meditation practice whose title could be translated as "Recommending Zazen for All People." Dogen suggested meditation (zazen, in Zen parlance) could be practiced universally.

What would it mean for everyone to practice meditation? Perhaps it sounds like a utopian fantasy; on the other hand, seeing how popular mindfulness meditation has become, it may be a case of "be careful what you wish for."

The zazen that Dogen recommended was not, he said, merely a technique of meditation, but rather, the Dharma gate of joy and ease. Passing through that gate was dependent on foregoing all our usual assumptions about meditation being a "technique," whether for attaining calmness, equanimity, or even enlightenment itself. But if meditation is not a technique, what is it? This is the question we see the mindfulness movement bypassing in its rush to transplant an explicit set of "techniques" taken from the practices of ascetic, renunciant Southeast Asian Theravadin Buddhist monastics, stripping them of their Buddhist and Asian origins, and repackaging them in a secularized and often medicalized guise for Westerners. The movement often contends that spiritual or religious experience can no longer make a convincing claim for the time and attention of the average person; instead, it insists a scientifically validated problem-focused method is required.

The mass media are noisy with the promises of what mindfulness will help you achieve; you can find mindfulness programs ranging from how to cope with cancer to how to learn to play the harmonica. Fascination with "mindfulness" has become so widespread it has become a generic term that can mean any of the following, to name just a few:

- a method for stress reduction
- a method of meditation
- a way of focusing and paying attention
- being alert instead of spacing out
- a method for controlling thoughts and feelings
- a method for training the brain

- a treatment for physical illness
- a method of psychotherapy
- a way of being kind and compassionate
- a path for personal happiness
- focusing on the present moment

We have no doubt that many, many people have benefitted from their exposure to mindfulness. Surely the practice of meditation, in whatever form, provides some help in developing a greater sense of equanimity in the face of the stresses of modern life. To the extent mindfulness helps people realize thoughts are just thoughts and sensations are just sensations, it is likely to be useful in clinical contexts for patients caught in cycles of physical pain and emotional suffering. Perhaps mindfulness can even, as some of its adherents claim (or at least hope), foster cooperation and peace between peoples—at least if it is offered in the context of an ethic of interdependence and nonviolence.

But bringing what had hitherto been an esoteric practice within reach of millions is not without both its pitfalls and pratfalls. Whenever something has the power to help, it will inevitably also have the power to harm; it could not otherwise be effective. There is no medication that doesn't cause side effects in some people; there is no solution that doesn't create unexpected consequences.

Paying attention is good but can be exhausting; being able to focus is good but sometimes comes at the expense of constricting creativity. Being alert is prized by society, but a good rest is important to restore and refresh. Self-awareness can help guide us or can make us awkwardly self-critical. Surely personal happiness is desirable, but can it be complete without taking into account others' happiness as well? And if we engage in a practice out of a desire for personal gain, can't that very desire ensnare us? Dogen may have recommended universal zazen, but he also said that realization is *effort without desire.*[1]

As mindfulness gets absorbed into a society that runs on the engines of consumerism, competition, and glorification of the individual self, it runs the danger of turning into one more brand trademarked for purely personal gratification. One might say that these trends illustrate all too well that self-involvement is not the same as self-awareness. A lot of good is coming from mindfulness practices, but a lot of money is being made as it becomes commercialized. Can a meditation that was developed within Buddhism—which teaches that desire lies at the core of suffering—be transformed into a convenient means to achieving a desired end without losing some of its heart? Can a spiritual practice become a commodity without suffering some effects? For that matter, when one secularizes the spiritual, does the change in context inevitably change the experience?

CONTRIBUTORS' PERSPECTIVES

Each contributor to this book offers a unique perspective on what "mindfulness" means in contemporary American Buddhism: these run the gamut from a deeply respectful reclaiming of the profound Theravadin roots of mindfulness, to deeply critical assessments of the dilution, if not outright perversion, of meditation presented shorn of its ethical and spiritual dimensions.

The first section of this book explores some of the potential risks of this secularization. The chapter by Marc Poirier, for instance, delves into how the intrusion of the marketplace into the practice of mindfulness can have myriad unintended side effects. Robert Rosenbaum offers a chapter investigating how the very word "mindfulness" can lead us to conceptualize mind in a narrow fashion, leading to a reification that misses the transformative Buddhist implications of the emptiness of all phenomena.

The chapter by Barry Magid and Marc Poirier examines the way their own Zen tradition is being transformed by trends dating back to the modernizing impulses of Meiji-era Japan. Magid is himself an example of a lay, nonmonastically trained, psychoanalyst Zen teacher; he and Poirier wonder how we can best establish a viable middle way between a return to traditional monastic training and the watering down of Buddhism they see taking place in the mindfulness movement. They suggest the tendency toward deracination, secularization, and instrumentalization that has characterized much of Buddhism's encounter with contemporary Western society has been taken to extremes by the mindfulness movement.

Following up on some of the points made earlier by Poirier, Robert Rosenbaum offers an overview of how the scientific evidence used to justify mindfulness practice can encourage a naive materialism whose boosterism ignores important conceptual and methodological difficulties. Hozan Alan Senauke raises a series of issues, concerned about what can occur when mindfulness is offered as a technique without being anchored in a set of ethical precepts. Finally, Sallie Jiko Tisdale describes, with considerable amusement, her experience as a Zen practitioner encountering some of the New Age attitudes that can accompany mass-market versions of mindfulness.

The second section describes some of the positive possibilities that can arise when Zen and mindfulness inform each other.

The Vipassana tradition of mindfulness remains a rich and fertile ground that many Zen teachers find fruitful to cultivate alongside their own practices. Gil Fronsdal and Max Erdstein describe how the original sutras treat mindfulness not as a meditation technique but as a basic mental faculty that is developed through being ardent, fully aware of our experience, and "putting away covetousness and grief for the world." They describe how they've integrated mindfulness and Zen, and some of what they've experienced as a result.

Norman Fischer offers us a poem and then reflects on the process of its composition. He depicts mindfulness as a kind of "negative capability" that enables him to write without any idea of what the poem would be; the poem can reach out from its own nonexistence, and he can be the vehicle for its coming into another order of being.

For some, issues of deep concern need to be brought within the circle of mindful awareness, lest the crucial dimensions of the political, the social, and the ethical remain dissociated from Zen practice. For Janet Jiryu Abels, for instance, "mindfulness" describes the bridge that joined "doing environmental stuff" with a deep practice-centered sense of interconnectedness. Similarly, Grace Schireson brought her practice off the cushion to directly question the treatment of women in Japanese Zen, even while she remained deeply immersed in sesshin retreat practice and koan study.

Sojun Mel Weitsman offers us a concrete example of Zen mindfulness.

Rather than describe an esoteric inquiry into modes of consciousness or psychological self-control, he takes us through how he makes an avocado sandwich while being fully present and aware. This is his personal expression of the Zen of everyday life—Layman Pang's "chopping wood and carrying water" for the twenty-first century urban resident. Everything we need is found in being just this moment. What could be lacking? This is in keeping with the Zen mode of mindfulness: nothing special. Ordinary mind is the Way.

A common theme in this second section is that mindfulness is not some technique to be practiced—an idea that paradoxically runs the danger of separating us from our experience—but is a plunging fully into our activities while letting go completely. In a sense, a lifetime of practice helps us forget "practices" completely. Instead of practicing mindfulness to get a handle on our experience, the faculty of mindfulness can help us get out of the way so we can let the experience inform us. As Sojun puts it in the final essay in this section, "the terrain is teaching me how to walk on it if I pay attention." We can trust the path that is laid down by walking.

Finally, in the epilogue Robert Sharf provides an analysis of the current tendency to equate Buddhist practice with meditation, meditation with mindfulness, and mindfulness with therapeutic psychological practice. He locates the origin of mindfulness meditation in the relatively recent past (the early twentieth century), placing it in the context of social and political factors affecting Theravadin Buddhism at that time, and alerts us to some of the ensuing ethical and ideological issues raised subsequently from both inside and outside the Buddhist community. Sharf's scholarly exegesis offers a valuable contextualization that illuminates the preceding chapters by our Zen authors.

Amid the many twists and turns Buddhism takes in coming to the West, its truths flow into a myriad of pathways. We are on a kind of pilgrimage; each essay in this book takes one step, but we don't know where the path will take us. We still are in the dark about where many of the pathways are heading: which will be enriching, which debasing, which will transform our culture at its most basic levels, and how that culture will in turn transform the traditional teachings.

In the face of uncertainty, some find conviction in the dogmas of religious belief, while some gain confidence in the concrete evidence of scientific studies. Others embrace the deep spiritual doubt that engenders great faith or the scientific skepticism that questions research results to widen the scope of inquiry and expand our sense of wonder. Standing at a crossroads, perhaps we can take a hint from a koan in the *Book of Serenity*:

Dizang asked Fayan, "Where are you going?"
Fayan said, "Around on pilgrimage."
Dizang said, "What is the purpose of pilgrimage?"
Fayan said, "I don't know."
Dizang said, "Not knowing is most intimate."[2]

PART I

CRITICAL CONCERNS

1. MISCHIEF IN THE MARKETPLACE FOR MINDFULNESS

Marc R. Poirier

As we desire the natural order
of our minds to be free from clinging,
. we must be aware of our greed.
—From the traditional Zen meal chant,
as interpreted at Ordinary Mind Zendo

These days there is a wide-open market for mindfulness training, of that there can be no doubt. And a market is made up of consumers, not practitioners in any traditional sense.

Generally speaking, consumers are driven by desire and aversion. Those who buy a good or service can be expected to inform themselves before making a purchase (to a certain extent, at least—information is costly); to compare products; to buy one and, if dissatisfied, then switch to another or look for substitutes that will achieve the same goals by other means; and to seek out the best price for value. When something stops being useful, you stop buying it. These are normal, value-maximizing behaviors.

From the supplier side, whatever label or design will enhance the value or marketability of a product or service is fair game. The goal is to sell product. There is much leeway about how one can brand a product. And what the consumer ultimately does with a product is not the producer's responsibility. The supplier sells, but he or she does not have an obligation to provide follow-up guidance or counsel. The consumer's desire guides all. Once you take meditation off the cushion—out of its original religious context—and bring it as "mindfulness" into the marketplace, it appears that just about anything can be labeled and linked to mindfulness one way or another.

This commodification of mindfulness and meditation is increasingly prevalent and problematic for a variety of reasons. It obscures the importance of at least three key aspects of traditional Buddhist training: (1) a sustained commitment to practice over time; (2) the usefulness of a community of practice in stabilizing and expanding individual practice; and (3) the importance of guidance from a learned and trusted teacher or elder with whom the student develops a long-term disciple relationship. These three elements are essential for those who wish to explore more deeply what mindfulness and meditation can offer as a way of life.

People will always flit in and out of meditation and mindfulness training. When sampling becomes the norm, however, and when supposedly skilled teachers offer nothing more than a few weeks of occasional practice undertaken in order to obtain a short-term anodyne, there is mischief afoot in the marketplace for mindfulness. In this chapter, I explore some characteristics of this mischief, first from the teacher side and then from the confused student side. I also comment on the pros and cons of relying on the rhetoric of science to validate and market mindfulness. Finally, I discuss the core issue: greed's central function in the marketplace and the importance of being aware of greed in a sustained Zen meditation practice.

A terminological note. I thought at first that it might be helpful to put blame on the widespread use of "mindfulness" these days in every possible context. But some skillful teachers use the word "mindfulness" to translate or expound in English what I view as credible Westernized interpretations of traditional Buddhist teachings: Joseph Goldstein, Bhante Gunaratana, and Bhikkhu Bodhi all offer a canonical perspective on mindfulness. At the same time, some current teachers of "meditation" offer it in ways quite foreign to the Zen practice I teach, as a technique to achieve a goal. So I will tend to talk about the two together; "meditation" as a more focused and ritualized practice of attention, and "mindfulness" as an extension of that attention into everyday life. The key question is whether mindfulness and meditation are deployed to explore and investigate and participate and behold—or instead to help an imagined separate self achieve gain and avert loss.

MISCHIEF IN THE TEACHING OF MINDFULNESS AND MEDITATION

Approaching practice as a goal-oriented technique has troubling consequences. Although a teacher might present specific practices as tools in the service of the relief of suffering or as a skillful means to engage students at the level of their most immediate concerns, when this advertisement for meditation is presented without even an occasional acknowledgment of the practices' links to wider, deeper, more transformative experiences and to the availability of accumulated wisdom in various traditions, the instructor does a disservice to the student, patient, or client. The wider road will not always be cut off, of course. In our information-rich culture, those who seek for more have many opportunities to find it, and Buddhist centers are no longer scarce. Still, I do not view offering meditation or mindfulness solely as a technique to a specific gain to be skillful.

The typical reply is that the practice will take care of itself. Just get folks to sit for a bit. At some point, presumably, the beginning student will find dissatisfaction inevitable, and he or she will back away from a results-based conception of what practice is about and begin to engage in an ongoing, wide-ranging inquiry with less thought of gain. But in my view, discovery of the profundities of practice is less likely to happen when the teacher articulates practice only in terms of short-term gain. Instead, the disappointed beginner will simply flit away, deciding to shop elsewhere.

A related issue concerns the background and length of practice experience of those who hold themselves out to be teachers of an instrumental view of mindfulness training. I have encountered a number of well-meaning professionals who have read about the benefits of mindfulness and meditation for lawyers and other professionals, in popular journals, books, or clinical reports. They may have dipped into an online course or a few weeks of practice. With just about no experience of what can happen in the course of a sustained practice, these folks then set out to provide workshops for others. They may find support from well-meaning institutions such as universities and bar associations, which also may have only a cursory and goal-oriented approach to mindfulness. Such instructors and institutions view mindfulness and meditation as easy-to-convey techniques, to be taught in a few days or weeks, often for a fee. Their lack of experience may seem to them of little concern, because they understand the techniques to be simple mechanisms with predictable results, as established by scientific studies.

All in all, I view this development as harmful. Many beginning practitioners will be guided to the shallow end of the pool. Worse, some of them may experience insights or rushes of psychological turmoil that an inexperienced instructor may be ill-equipped to address or perhaps even to recognize. Well-constructed training programs that provide ongoing support can address some of the issues of a new teacher's inexperience. But those who offer to teach practices that they themselves have acquired in an off-handed way may well not seek out the appropriate training to help them support their students—especially if they view what they are doing as a business, not a professional commitment.

This incorporation of instruction in mindfulness and meditation in institutional contexts such as corporations and law firms is very concerning. Such projects purport to be about the well-being and happiness of workers but are skewed in a direction of increasing productivity and marketable creativity. Google's Search Inside Yourself project is an example. Starting in its title, it purports to promise "success, happiness (and world peace)." Google has just completed its first training of a group of independent trainers. They will use Google's brand and corporate cachet to market mindfulness training to major businesses. A graduate of Google's Search Inside Yourself program "considers it as sort of an organizational WD-40, a necessary lubricant between driven, ambitious employees and Google's demanding corporate culture."[1]

One recent *New York Times* article assessed Google's approach (approvingly, I might add) as teaching employees "to recognize and accept inner thoughts and feelings rather than ignore or repress them," which is "in the company's interest because it frees up employees' otherwise embattled brain space to intuit end users' desires and create products to satisfy them."[2] I object. This paradigm is especially insidious, as neither the sponsor nor the instructor is interested in the student exploring the free play of awareness. The instructor and the corporate sponsor have a stake in avoiding valorizing the experience of unsatisfactoriness. It is contrary to the employer's goal of achieving more productive workers and to the instructors' pitch to those workers that practice will make them happy and successful.

I have somewhat fewer qualms about the widespread adoption of mindfulness practices in healthcare and medical school contexts. This very important development is due in large part to decades of effort by Jon Kabat-Zinn's Mindfulness-Based Stress Reduction (MBSR) program at the Center for Mindfulness in Medicine, Health Care, and Society, based at the University of Massachusetts Medical School. A core ethical expectation of healing, or at least doing no harm, pervades the health care professions, keeping the interests of institutions, mindfulness instructors, and patients more or less aligned. So Kabat-Zinn's very successful secularization of Buddhist practices is protected from the worst effects of commodification, to some extent, by a preexisting professional ethos in the health care fields; they also have developed a certification process for their instructors.

There is no similar secular ethical constraint that pervades the worlds of business and law. Maximizing productivity or wealth is about as close as one can come, and that's not a good foundation for undertaking practice.[3] Sooner or later, conflicts of interest are likely to arise when the consultant on mindfulness or meditation, who works for or is hired by the employer, works with employees as they discover roots of unhappiness in their work situation. Is the instructor's allegiance to the employer or to the employee? Without a much clearer ethical code for secular instruction, I expect that serious harm will be done from time to time by instructors whose own financial interest is aligned with keeping executives in large corporations happy with results. In business contexts, the notion that mindfulness will produce happier, more productive employees is simply at odds with exploring some of the roots of life's unsatisfactoriness.

Contemplative practices are also being systematically introduced into educational contexts.[4] The circumstances and uses are quite varied. I don't take a strong position on the use of these techniques to encourage youth to notice more deeply and to explore their intuitions. That's legitimate education. One must wonder again here whether extended practice might present situations beyond the skill of an inexperienced instructor. No doubt, as some studies show, introducing mindfulness training in middle schools and high schools can reduce violence. But will the instructor be equipped for other consequences of young students engaging in mindfulness practice?

At the college level, young adults may well be looking for practices that will develop a sustained inquiry such as Zen practice. Hopefully these settings will provide resources for those moved to go further.

In professional contexts, such as the law school setting with which I am familiar, mindfulness training is typically being offered as stress-reduction and balance, in order to offset the acknowledged deleterious psychological effects of law school and the practice of law.[5] As I've said throughout this chapter, that approach is unfortunate.

Some law professors do tie the value of skills developed through meditation and mindfulness techniques to lawyering competencies, especially in the areas of mediation and negotiation; Clark Freshman, for instance, argues that mindfulness training enables one to detect lying.[6] But others argue that emotional intelligence, not contemplative practice, develops these competencies.[7] Sometimes mindfulness is studied formally in law school, as part of a course on emotional intelligence, or in order to appreciate the role it may play in the successful practice of law. It is still all very instrumental, very take-it-or-leave-it. Only occasionally do voices in legal education go further, gesturing toward the authenticity and groundedness that a contemplative practice can offer the lawyer;[8] describing meditation as a source of long-term satisfaction;[9] or emphasizing the importance to the practice of law of teaching students to access a further spiritual and ethical dimension through contemplative practice.[10]

MISCHIEF FROM THE STUDENT'S SIDE

Beginning students almost always seek out instruction in a meditation or mindfulness practice because of personal pain or loss, the sense something is lacking, or a need to fix some aspect of their life. Occasionally, they wish to become enlightened. Consequently, impatience with unsatisfactory results, flightiness, and misunderstanding of how deep change in one's life occurs are common aspects of a beginner's practice. An encouragement to stay put and stick with it are essential to a skillful introduction to practice, helping it to ripen over time.

In my own life, after reading Philip Kapleau's exhortations about sustained practice in *The Three Pillars of Zen*, I sought out a local Zen center and, after one evening's experience, wrote out on a scrap of paper a commitment to practice Zen for ten years, after which it would be permissible to move on. That piece of paper stayed posted on my bedroom mirror for a decade. This was a little extreme, I admit, and I did not know what I was getting into, in more than one sense. Still, my own slogans for teaching law students and professionals who are too busy to sit captures some of this need to emphasize commitment: Show up, slow down, step back, settle in.

Workshop mentality and commodification are hindrances here. As Barry Magid argues, part of the function of sustained practice is gradually to attenuate the "curative fantasy" that beginners bring to practice, so as to allow the ripening of a kind of appreciation for life as it is, including especially its unsatisfactoriness and impermanence.[11] When the beginner's notion of gain is unexamined and even encouraged by commodification and instrumentalization, the student's exploration of unsatisfactoriness may be postponed, perhaps permanently.

I can do no better here than point to the description of her investigation of mindfulness provided by Gretchen Rubin in her book *The Happiness Project*. Rubin was editor-in-chief of the *Yale Law Journal*, clerked for Supreme Court Justice Sandra Day O'Connor, and worked for a prestigious law firm. After leaving the practice of law, she wrote two well-received if unconventionally structured biographies. Smart and accomplished she surely is. At the age of forty, she decided to make her life happier. After doing considerable research on the science of happiness (as a Supreme Court clerk, systematic and wide research is a role she is clearly comfortable in), she discerned fifteen principles that lead to happiness. Then she divided the year up into twelve month-long projects, and set up a blog so that her followers could discover along with her how to achieve happiness.

October was to be the month for mindfulness, Buddhism, and paying attention. Unfortunately, Ms. Rubin found herself unable to set aside fifteen minutes a day to sit quietly, and so she resorted to post-it notes with messages reminding her of the state of mind she meant to achieve through meditation, so that she could will herself into that state throughout the day. When that approach did not work, she sought out a hypnotist, so that she could just skip over the effort of having to do a straightforward, simple meditation practice every day for a month. Rubin also explored koan study, which seemed more interesting to her than meditation; but she decided to choose her own koans rather than explore traditional Zen ones. Rubin's month of exploring mindfulness also including keeping a food diary, laughter yoga, taking a drawing class to stimulate underutilized parts of her brain, listening to music (ABBA) as a mindfulness practice, and reexamining her habitual rules and expectations. A busy time! In November she moved on to "cram in everything [she] hadn't covered" earlier in the year, focusing on attitude and keeping a contented heart.[12]

Rubin's attempts to engage practice are surely misguided. They exemplify the hindrance of restlessness. She researches well, but then bypasses traditional forms of meditation practice, inventing her own. Having found practice unsatisfactory after a few days, she throws in the towel and moves on.

It is also significant that Rubin shopped alone. She taught herself her practice without the guidance of an elder or teacher or the support of peers in a sangha, a practice community. She composed for herself a composite of various traditions, which she tasted and rejected within a month—which is all the time she left herself. All these missteps contributed to her going sadly astray. Perhaps just as unfortunate, she blogged about all this. She has many followers who may well look to her example of how to engage and abandon a practice.

Now, there is nothing wrong with a beginner wandering for a while, exploring various teachers and traditions, and then settling in. I personally spent the 1980s doing this, even while my Zen practice was also deepening. But the practices explored should have an expectation of eventual commitment; a practice group or congregation or sangha; and a teacher, elder, or guide.

There is a symbiosis between the beginner's restlessness and teachers who play to the idea of gain through meditation. Scott Rogers's advice to lawyers in *The Six-Minute Lawyer*, and his similar advice in similar short books for law students, judges, and so on, reproduces several authentic practices, but in a context where the reader is encouraged to pick and choose, much as he or she might take aspirin for an occasional headache. And of course the whole endeavor need not take more than six minutes a day. Similar quickie approaches can be found in many contexts.[13]

The eight-week training format originated by Jon Kabat-Zinn in Mindfulness-Based Stress Reduction (MBSR) is comparatively skillful in this sense, for it is long enough to provide the beginner a valid first encounter with a variety of practices. In the MBSR course I took, participants were encouraged to commit forty-five minutes a day to a series of contemplative practices, six days a week. That's a good start toward establishing a habit. MBSR's eight-week format now reappears in studies and in many other kinds of modular training.[14]

One issue with the modular format is that it may drop students at the end of the eight weeks with a goodbye wave, a wish of good luck, and perhaps a list of practice opportunities—many of them, in my experience, Buddhist or Buddhist-inspired centers. So regardless of its merits, an eight-week modular training structure can facilitate a perception that eight weeks of practice suffice. Sustained engagement in practice is supported by a relationship with a teacher, a sangha, and a place of practice. Eight-week modules provide none of these.

It is possible to construct a sequence of instruction that begins with short modules that lead those who find some value there to longer practice periods, and eventually to a sustained relationship with a teacher and a sangha. My experience with the Shambhala training in the 1980s reflected that approach. There the workshop model was used at the front end, but there was a door beyond it leading into a structure more supportive of sustained practice.

I must mention here that some MBSR teachers are organizing structures and courses that respond to these concerns. For example, in the New York City area, a Mindfulness Collaborative comprised of MBSR instructors states, as part of its mission, "the development of innovative curricula grounded in the 8-week MBSR cycle as pioneered by Jon Kabat-Zinn and the Center for Mindfulness."[15] Some teachers in this group go beyond the eight-week format by offering monthly sitting groups or series of classes on aspects of mindfulness as taught by MBSR. So in this particular geographic area, MBSR teachers are exploring reintroducing some of the structure that was tailored out of the eight-week module. How widespread this retailoring is I do not know. To the extent that it solidifies into habitual longer-term structures as part of MBSR, it seems to me to be a movement back toward a religion-like frame within which to secure practice.

One of the more insidious aspects of commodified mindfulness is that it validates the practitioner's pursuit of happiness[16]—recall that Rubin's book is entitled *The Happiness Project*. "Happiness" is a tricky premise. Barry Magid has authored an introduction to Zen practice entitled *Ending the Pursuit of Happiness* precisely to underscore the futility of undertaking a Zen practice in the hope of actualizing a curative fantasy. Other teachers hold out some sort of happiness as a way of encouraging folks to begin practice, though some of these, when read carefully, don't promise the kind of happiness Rubin sought, only a relative familiarity and contentment with life's ever-changing quality: Ezra Bayda in his *Beyond Happiness*, for instance. This is a more sensible and honest approach. As Barry Magid pointed out, rather than being a particular subjective state of mind we seek to cultivate, happiness is perhaps best understood the way Aristotle did, as eudaemonia—the "flourishing" that results from a lifetime of cultivating our virtues and capacities.

All in all, I question the skillfulness of too much talk about happiness, as it seems only further to entangle beginning students in their misconceptions and self-deceptions regarding the nature of practice and of life.

A FEW OBSERVATIONS ABOUT THE SCIENCE RHETORIC

One important development of the past few decades has been the wave of scientific studies on various aspects and effects of mindfulness and meditation. Only a few years ago, there was but a trickle of studies, many of them funded by proponents of particular techniques such as Transcendental Meditation or MBSR. Now there may be four to five hundred new studies a year.[17] Many well-respected research universities have major projects studying clinical applications, behavioral effects, and, in the last decade or so, neurophysiological patterns as they are affected by mindfulness and meditation practices.

To some extent, this scientific turn is welcome. It is a technique of secular legitimation. Science provides a basis to verify claims of the benefits of mindfulness and meditation and can be used to encourage the skeptical to dip their toes into a practice. Science, not a cult or a suspect human authority figure, tells us that it works. As one law student recently expressed to me, the scientific data gives him the faith to engage a mindfulness practice. This is an interesting juxtaposition of science and faith. I don't purport here to sort through the burgeoning science literature, to parse the good studies from the weaker ones, or to put a fine point on how meditation techniques can be put to use (see instead, perhaps, Bob Rosenbaum's chapter "Mindfulness Myths" in this book). Given the volume of the studies, that would be a life's work. And I do not mean to gainsay what are clearly effective and useful therapeutic applications of meditation and mindfulness techniques, whether for stress reduction, treatment of grief and depression, improvement of focus, pain management, or some physical illnesses.

I do have some difficulty with the current claims for the benefits of mindfulness and meditation when based on neuroscience.[18] Changes in brain activity or structure, one lobe lighting up more after a few weeks of meditation, is curious and interesting and perhaps important, but doesn't in itself get at any of what is going on from the point of view of the practitioner's experience or understanding. The brain is not the self. Brain science does not describe the experience of meditation or mindfulness in a way that can be used to help guide the practitioner's explorations. Neither the neuroscience literature nor the clinical psychology literature begins to approach the descriptive richness or the compassionate wisdom that is sometimes articulated by Buddhist teachers, ancient and modern. Scientific studies are moreover no substitute for the tailored support for practice provided by competent and experienced teachers, a well-functioning sangha, and traditional ritual and wisdom. In a fundamental sense, the science is disconnected from meditative experience and practice and teaching, even as it seeks to investigate it. It is a different endeavor altogether.

The law student who found science a source of faith in his practice had something interesting to say about this. I asked if he engaged in a sport, and he turned out to be a runner. But, he pointed out, although he knew about physiological and psychological effects of long-distance running, he did not engage in his sport because of them. He did not think about generating endorphins when he experienced running. His running was a long-term habit that made him feel a certain way and that was part of his life. Why did he run? He just does. Why do I put on my robe at the sound of the bell? I do.

A more problematic aspect to scientific justifications for mindfulness practice is that they reinforce the model of gain from practice. Much of the therapeutic literature incorporating and communicating the science as it develops does so in the service of goal achievement, potentially obscuring the fundamental practice of just sitting. The definition of valid scientific work is to present results that can be reproduced. Pure science feeds into applied science, and both partake of a basic frame of usefulness and goal achievement and the predictable manipulation of events. That's important in its sphere. But to justify meditation and mindfulness on the grounds that neuroscience is beginning to be able to establish reproducible results only serves to distance the practitioner from the kind of practice I recommend.

Even more problematic, the science is eagerly appropriated and repurposed by marketers. I've heard many a pitch for mindfulness that includes some dumbed-down version of its effects on neuroplasticity, the amygdala, the left prefrontal lobe, the hippocampus, the vagus nerve, and so on. Often the invocation of science is linked to rather large promises of goal achievement—try this for a few weeks because look at what it does to your brain! By peddling so hard the usefulness of meditation as technique, these approaches can obscure the basic Zen practice of just being, with its experience of noticing, stillness, and occasional joy.

JUST SITTING: NO GREED AND NO END OF GREED

Commodification and instrumentalization of practice are widespread. They are inevitable, because we are human. We will not be rid of them or of the greed that underlies them. Indeed, in everyday life, we must function in a world of this-and-that, picking and choosing, getting and spending.

In contrast, just sitting serves as the occasion, the regular time and place, of a practice of nonpursuing. Results do arise from just sitting—yet they are byproducts. Ideas around those results, framing them as goals, will also arise, stimulating recurring tendrils of greed and aversion. On the cushion, these events are noted, and one then returns to just sitting. For the experienced practitioner, more and more, instead of holding meditation and mindfulness to be a tool to shape daily life, practice becomes a habitual container of encounter, a nonjudgmental practice of "now what?" within which daily life off the cushion is held. Then we say to those reoccuring tendrils not "Oh, no!" but "Now what?"

This appreciation of clinging, one might notice, is very much the same process as Dogen's basic instruction for just sitting: "Think not-thinking. What is not thinking? Nonthinking."[19] Dogen was not pointing to the suppression of thought, but rather to allowing thoughts and sensations to arise and fall, noting their insubstantial nature more and more deeply. If one approaches "not-thinking" in the purposive sense of suppression of some activity one is not supposed to be doing, then one is still "doing" something during sitting practice. That "doing" is "done" by a separate, active "self" that picks and chooses—and off we go! Instead, just note thinking, take it in.

Not-thinking may sound odd as a use of "not." However, the same kind of "no" and "not" appear regularly in some core Zen texts. The "no" and the "emptiness" that are repeated throughout the Heart Sutra point to the effects of clearly seeing impermanence and interconnectedness—and thus misfortune and pain are shifted, transcended, not blotted out and replaced by goodies. "No path, no wisdom, no attainment; indeed there is nothing to be attained." No gain. No hindrance.

To allow thought to come and go, not suppressing it, not using meditation to bring about particular states of mind, even those of clarity or calmness, is to appreciate what is known as the "emptiness" of thought and mental states. This emptiness is not itself yet another state of consciousness. It is the underlying nature of all things, transient and thus "empty" of any unchanging essence. Since all thoughts, all dharmas, are already empty, meditation leaves everything exactly as it found it. What changes is our awareness of our compulsive, clinging- and fear-driven attempts to deny, avoid, or control the flow of consciousness, the flow of life. And ultimately that fear, along with everything, is part of the flow.

For all of us (or just possibly for all but the very most advanced), there is hindrance, there is continued craving. Hence, this chapter's epigraph, which comes from the traditional formal meal chant, as Ordinary Mind Zendo has adapted it. In this version, the sentence reads, "As we desire the natural order of our minds to be free from clinging, we must be aware of our greed."

A more traditional version would state, "We must be free from greed." But that formulation is a problem. It prefers one state (greed-free) over another (greedy). The tendrils of greed recur. This happens in a particularly clear form when one hasn't eaten lately and is sitting still during sesshin in front of three bowls of food and drink, I can assure you. But it happens all the time. Our best bet is not to pretend otherwise.

We can note desires without encouraging them. In my school of Zen, that is how we understand both a daily practice of just sitting and everyday Zen. Our version of the meal chant expresses simply that the two things occur simultaneously in practice—a desire to be free from clinging and an examination of our greed. Where am I stuck, where am I clinging? What are its shape and texture? Sitting with that inquiry may soften some of the habit of attachment. As Zen teacher Kosho Uchiyama wrote, Zen practice involves "opening the hand of thought."[20] Not to acknowledge our greed and aversion at all is being dishonest about our true nature, which does include those qualities, though it is not necessarily driven by them.

So I return to the problem of commodification and instrumentalization as a framing for mindfulness and meditation in the West. What is at stake, deeply at stake, is unexamined greed and aversion. "Do X and you may well get Y" as a premise for meditation and mindfulness leaves the particular kind of pain caused by greed and aversion unexplored.

The market ethos in fact depends on greed, unquestioningly. In the frenzied, short-term, workshop mode of mindfulness and meditation, tendrils of greed are watered and nurtured, rather than examined in a way that allows them naturally to settle out and dissipate. Meditation and mindfulness instructors who respond by marketing their products in a way claiming to offer some final satisfaction are stimulating greed and aversion, perhaps without even being aware of it. And they may themselves, if their own practice is short-term or shallow or disconnected from its Buddhist roots, not even be aware of the alternative mode described here.

Many benefits and fruits of Zen practice are real, but they are not to be gained, nor pursued. Just sit, regularly, for a sustained period, and see what is here right now.

2. "I" DOESN'T MIND

Robert Meikyo Rosenbaum

There is nothing in the triple world;
where can mind be found?[1]
—*Blue Cliff Record*, Koan #37

All practices are poison; they invoke the very problems they address. Solutions and problems, like all phenomena, are interdependent, inextricably intertwined; the cure must invoke the disease as surely as enlightenment can only be realized through delusion. Any meditation practice can become a poison, regardless of whether it's immersion in mindfulness, Zen koans, shikantaza ("just sitting"), or even exercises aimed at increasing compassion.

The practice of mindfulness may have a particular vulnerability that at first seems to be its strength: over the last few decades it has lent itself to extraction from its original Buddhist roots and been applied as a solution to a variety of modern ills. It can be used for stress reduction, to deal with medical problems, and as an adjunct to psychotherapy; it has been embraced by positive psychology proponents, New Age enthusiasts, and myriads of people interested in self-improvement. However, when mindfulness is taken out of its original Buddhist context and practiced as an isolated technique, it can lead to effects exactly the opposite of what were intended.

Mindfulness, according to a well-known introduction to the Satipatthana Sutta by Soma Thera,[2] is designed to liberate practitioners from suffering and craving by developing insight into the transience of all things and into their emptiness of self-essence. It helps us deconstruct the false sense of self that is the basis of delusion and suffering, and it aims at the liberation not just of ourselves but of all beings. If we use mindfulness merely to achieve a greater sense of personal well-being, or as a palliative technique to alleviate a painful experience, its effects are much more limited.

Some of the genuine value of mindfulness lies in the way it can increase what therapists call "ego strength": the ability to tolerate our emotions, maintain the ability to think flexibly, and respond with resilience to disappointments and challenging life circumstances. However, if mindfulness practice stops there it paradoxically can reinforce the false sense of an essential self—which from a Buddhist perspective is actually a primary source of our misery. The emphasis mindfulness places on awareness of the contents of mind can inculcate a sense of an "I" being mindful of an "it" and in doing so reinforce the very ego the practice is meant to shake up.

On the one hand, when "I" can be aware of "my" feelings as just feelings and "my" sensations as just sensations, "my observing ego" obtains some distance from the impulse and emotions that can overwhelm it. This apparently benign result, though, masks a potentially toxic seed: introducing a welcome distance from the vagaries of thoughts, feelings, perceptions, and impulses also can produce a divisive sense of separation.

It's nice to not feel at the mercy of one's feelings and sensations, but if "I" am separate from "my" emotions and thoughts and physical experience, what do "I" *really* feel and believe? Who is this "I" that is being aware? When mindfulness practice is shorn of its Buddhist teachings, it offers no method for addressing this essential existential question. This may lead to people basing their sense of self on an insecure attachment to some particular mental state or badge of identity. We can even become attached to the practice of mindfulness itself: "I" am the person who practices mindfulness.

This is dangerous: it can lead to the sense that "I" am the one who is responsible for "creating" mindful mental states. Instead of just watching mental states come and go, I may try overmuch to control them. Instead of feeling gratitude at recognizing mindfulness as a basic human faculty, I may feel I am both the author and the owner of "my" mindfulness.

This can be an effortful burden. If I lapse in being mindful, I may feel like a failure and berate myself. Alternatively I might place the blame on external circumstances being too difficult (but the most difficult situations are precisely when we need to be most mindful) or even blame others ("he isn't being mindful enough... he really did attack me... I needed to drop mindfulness and defend myself"). The opposite holds true as well; if we succeed in cultivating mindfulness we can feel good about our accomplishment and subtly set ourselves apart from, and feel slightly superior to, other "nonmindful" friends, associates, and family members. We might even become mindfulness professionals and think we have something special to teach others!

This is a well-known trap in almost any practice that leads to mastery of a skill. In Zen, it's an almost inevitable stage commonly seen in enthusiastic beginners, but we are warned against it: we say of such a person that "he stinks of Zen." We are taught to not cling to any one method (even the Buddhadharma), experience (even enlightenment), or fixed sense of who we are. This includes letting go of "mind" itself. Thus a famous Zen koan:

> Damei Fachang of Ming Province asked Mazu Daoyi,
>   "What is buddha?"
> Mazu answered,
>   "This very mind is buddha."
> Later another monk asked Mazu,
>   "What is buddha?"
> The master replied,
>   "Not mind, not buddha."[3]

Liberation comes from letting go of everything, since every *thing* is, basically, empty of any essence. This is difficult, so Buddhism has many skillful means to assist the process. The Satipatthana Sutta, the central text on the way of mindfulness, does not stop with mindfulness of breathing, modes of deportment, and clear comprehension; in order to liberate the practitioner from attachment and clinging, it goes on to encourage the practitioner to reflect on the repulsiveness of the body, on the rotting corpses in a cemetery, and on the fragmentary nature of all materiality. This doesn't initially feel very comforting, so it rarely forms part of the instruction in secularized, goal-oriented self-improvement courses on mindfulness.

But radical letting go is a key to liberation. In Buddhist practice, as we let go of our hold, we start to realize "I" am not the one who produces mindfulness. Rather, as Joseph Goldstein and Jack Kornfield describe, when we stop "doing" anything and allow ourselves to sink deeper into stillness, "We see in the depths of our being how nothing at all lasts and nothing can be grasped… 'No self, no problem!'… We come to a ground of silence as inherent completeness… and freedom of our being emerges and expresses itself naturally."[4]

Zen teacher Shunryu Suzuki used to say that it is a big mistake to think that you are the one who meditates. When we let the meditation do the meditating, it is effortless effort; we are the expression of something larger than ourselves (but which can only be expressed through each being's practice). In Zen we say "I am not It; It actually is me."[5] But when mindfulness (or any meditation) is taught purely as a technique I can master, it can become a source of false pride.

Pride is not a sin, but it can restrict our sense of wonder to an unnecessarily narrow field.

GRASPING AT MIND

Another danger in practicing mindfulness is inherent in the very word. "Mindfulness" sounds like there is a wise "mind" that "I" can be full of, and that "I" should be able to access. Many classes on mindfulness teach that there is a "conscious" mind (often associated with thought), an "unconscious" mind (often associated with feeling), and a "wise" mind that resides at the intersection of the two. This reification is misleading; it can lead me to try to control my mind so it is always "full" of "wise mind." This can be a problem, as exemplified in another well-known koan:

Dazu Huike: Master, I cannot pacify my mind. Please help me.
Bodhidharma: Bring me that mind, and I will pacify it for you.
Dazu Huike: When I search my mind I cannot hold it, so I can't bring it to you.
Bodhidharma: Now your mind is pacified.[6]

Zen delights in paradoxes, partially because they're fun, but more importantly because they reflect the world as it truly is: wondrous mystery, streaming and shimmering. Neither the mind nor anything in the world stays still long enough for us to be able to grasp it. Perhaps it is better to say the world's stillness rests on movement, and its movement rests on stillness: moment to moment, constant flow.

Vipassana mindfulness practice intentionally introduces a split between the observer and the observed, breaking down consciousness and the objects of consciousness so that the meditator discovers both are merely "heaps" of transient components, or *skandhas*. Zen practice, while acknowledging the value of mindfulness, also is marked by a strong sense that using mind to control mind is a big mistake, one that leads to infinite levels of recursiveness. You can be aware of being aware, and aware of being aware of being aware, and aware of being aware of being aware of being aware, and so on. The problem is (to use a common Zen phrase) that the eye cannot see itself. If you only go from room to room looking out for your glasses, you may fail to notice they are perched on your head.

Huangbo, an influential ninth-century Zen teacher, described the problem this way:

> When people hear that all buddhas transmit the Dharma of the Mind, they fantasize that there is a special Dharma they might attain; they suppose that there is something to be acquired or realized apart from Mind. They then try to use Mind to seek the Dharma, not knowing that Mind and the object of their search are one; they don't realize that this very Mind is the Dharma and that the Dharma is this very Mind.
>
> The mind cannot be used to seek the Mind; doing so through thousands and thousands of *kalpas* [eons] of cultivation, you will still not acquire It.[7]

Zen meditation focuses not so much on observation and insight (though it involves both) as on direct experience: immersion in nonstop flow. This experience is ungraspable, so when Zen Master Joshu was asked, "What is meditation?" he replied, "It is not meditation." Pressed further to describe meditation, Joshu simply responded, "It's *alive*."[8]

MOMENTS AND MINDFULNESS

Zen differs from mindfulness practice in placing less emphasis on training in modes of awareness. However, both practices share an interest in
presence.

In his essay "Actualizing the Fundamental Point," Zen Teacher Eihei
Dogen writes, "When you find your place where you are, practice occurs...
When you find your way at this moment, practice occurs... Here is the
place; here the way unfolds."[9] We can compare this to a commonly used
description of mindfulness by Jon Kabat-Zinn: "Paying attention in a particular way: on purpose, nonjudgmentally, in the present moment... mindfulness is about being fully awake in our lives, it is about perceiving the
exquisite vividness of each moment."[10]

Being fully alive here and now is a gift, what I like to call "the present of
presence." But there is a problem, which can be seen in the introduction to
koan number 28 from the Gateless Gate (*Wumenguan*):

> Deshan, a scholar of the Diamond Sutra, was traveling south to teach,
> carrying his commentaries on the Diamond Sutra with him. On the
> road he met an old woman selling tea and rice cakes, and told her he
> would like to buy some refreshments. After finding out who he was
> and what he was carrying, the old woman said to Deshan:
> "I will sell you some rice cakes if you can answer a question for me.
> In the Diamond Sutra it says that past mind is ungraspable, future
> mind is ungraspable, and present mind is ungraspable. What is the
> mind you wish to refresh with rice cakes and tea?"[11]

We know the past is gone and the future is not here yet. But the present
moment cannot be grasped. When I was in college, I read Ram Dass's *Be
Here Now* and spent a year meditating trying to be fully aware "right now."
It's not possible. (If you don't want to take my word for it, try it; you'll find
whenever you say "now" you're already too late.)

How, then, can we be "in" the present moment, as is sometimes taught
in classes on mindfulness-based stress reduction? Consider Dogen's Zen
response to this issue:

The way-seeking mind arises in a moment. A way-seeking moment arises in the mind... This is the understanding that the self is time.[12]

The self is time. The self is not a thing: it sparkles and ripples and moves. It's important not to identify with any of the myriad components that flash by, the bits and pieces that constitute us, however glorious they might appear. This is the central liberating teaching of Buddhism—there is no essential self, and we should not even become attached to identifying ourselves with our mind. Elsewhere Dogen explicitly says, "The mind is not I."[13]

When we are not attached to any particular mode of attention or consciousness, we can discover a vast intimacy in all being, not only in meditation but in everyday life.

UNDIVIDED ACTIVITY

Mindfulness meditation fosters liberation with a careful examination of the workings of the mind; by exploring the varieties of consciousness, awareness, and the objects of mind, one develops insight not only into the transience of all phenomena but also their basic freedom of any graspable essence. Dogen, though, in the process of establishing Soto Zen in thirteenth-century Japan, issued a warning: "The mind is able to make everything its object" but these varieties of mind "are not the teaching of the buddhas and ancestors."[14]

The problem is that when we treat something as an object we introduce a separation that obscures the continuously flowing, dynamic inter-being of all existence; then there seems to be a tangible essence to subject and object independent of each other. Zen encourages us to have a direct experience of the vibrant flow of being through the practice of what is sometimes called "the teaching of no-mind"; it includes meditation instructions such as "drop body and mind," and "think not-thinking." Thich Nhat Hanh, who encompasses aspects of both Zen and mindfulness traditions, describes meditative states characterized by no-mind: nonperception (where there is no perception and no need for perception; the meditator is present but does not perceive objects) and the attainment of cessation (where there is not only no perception but also no feelings, no cognition). He sees these states as crucial to a process of fundamental transformation that occurs through "the insight that the object it grasps is not self, and that subject and object are not separate but are one. We see ourselves in our universe, in other people, and in other species, and we see the universe and others in ourselves."[15]

The point here is that becoming more mindful only in the restricted sense of being "more attentive" of your surroundings and of your thoughts, emotions, and perceptions does not tap into the depths of meditation practice. Being "more attentive" while clinging to a sense of yourself as a separate, independent being will not necessarily make you a better person any more than solving a koan will prevent you from becoming depressed or completing a thousand prostrations will make it easier for you to drive to work in the morning. Conscious awareness can facilitate, but should not be mistaken for, enlightened being. Enlightened being requires seeing ourselves in others and others in ourselves: this is not a state of mind, not a refined consciousness, but a universe of continuous practice.

Zen meditation is a continuous practice of liberation not so much through observation and awareness—though it includes these—as through undivided activity in mundane, everyday experience. Zen prefers manifestation to observation and explanation; the prototype Zen example of Dharma transmission is Buddha holding up a flower and his disciple responding with a simple smile. Zen practice emphasizes a total immersion in the *suchness*, the "just this" of whatever presents itself, shorn as much as possible of self-centered views.

Rather than (or better said, *coexistent with*) paying attention to the workings of the individual self, Zen meditation encourages letting go of self; this is sometimes referred to as "dropping body and mind." Instead of standing apart one plunges in, and there is a kind of merging that "leaps beyond" self and object, many and one, even while including the specific particulars of each unique enactment.

BODY AND MIND STUDY OF THE WAY

When we meditate in this fashion, whatever realization we are graced with does not come as a lump of knowledge we acquire, grasp in our consciousness, and put in our storehouse. The more we become aware, the more we understand that realization comes forth naturally and simultaneously with its practice; our job is not to achieve realization but to put it into play while getting out of the way of its expression. It's nothing special. We just "assist the self-becoming of all being"[16] (including our own) without adding anything or taking anything away.

> Don't talk much about it;
> just work quietly at it.
> When the work has its fruit, allow people to say,
> "It just happened naturally."[17]

It's natural, then, to sometimes study the way with the body, sometimes with the mind; sometimes by casting off the mind, sometimes by taking up the mind. We study the way with thinking, and we study the way with "not-thinking."[18]

So when we're drinking a cup of tea, rather than focus (as in a common mindfulness exercise) on whether the sensations are pleasant, unpleasant, or neutral, rather than think about the chain of being that brought forth the tea plant and its harvest, perhaps we will instead simply immerse ourselves in the experience. Without thinking too much about it, we'll practice holding the cup with both hands, using just the right amount of grip strength, neither too tight nor too loose; we'll pour the tea *just so* without spilling a drop; we'll bow to the server and to the tea itself; we'll sip the tea without regard to whether we like it or not, but with full appreciation of the "suchness" of water and tea and cup and hands and lips. Doing this again and again, we let go of self-consciousness and intentional observation; we find ourselves where we are through forgetting ourselves in the act of drinking by merging with it. Then the tea realizes itself in being consumed, and we realize ourselves by consuming ourselves in the drinking of it.

Nurtured by the continuous mystery of the ordinary and the inexpressible wonder of the mundane, we do not gain anything but awe, we do not lose anything but self-importance. We do not practice in order to become enlightened, but to express the enlightenment that is every where and every when.

"Zen Mind" is drinking tea and sweeping the porch. It is bits and pieces that are undivided and whole in their ordinariness. Body and mind are two sides of the same coin, and both are found everywhere. As Dogen says, "Because the study of the way is like this, walls, tiles, and pebbles are mind... this human body, undivided by self and others, is the entire world." This very mind is always anchored in the immediacy of concrete experience:

> [It] is beyond one or two... it is free of error; it has thinking, sensing, mindfulness, and realization and it is free of thinking, sensing, mindfulness, and realization...
>> Blues, yellows, reds, and whites are the mind.
>> The long, the short, the square, and the round are the mind.
>> Living-and-dying and coming-and-going are the mind.
>> Years, months, days, and hours are the mind.
>> Dreams and fantasies, and flowers in space, are the mind.
>> The spray of water, foam, and flame are the mind.
>> Spring flowers and the autumn moon are the mind.
>> Each moment is the mind. *And yet it can never be broken* [my italics].[19]

Ultimately, we meditate to touch the wholeness of life that can never be broken. *Just this* flows constantly, whether we are aware of it or not. To help us realize *just this,* we cultivate modes of attention and consciousness that bring us down into our bones, to our way-seeking mind that is fully liberated precisely because it can never be grasped. The mind of *just this* is beyond attainment; it is the source of attention and its ultimate resting place.

For each of us the fundamental question is this:

At just this moment, what is it that appears directly in front of you?[20]

Mind cannot objectify it; thinking cannot describe it.[21]

3. THE THREE SHAKY PILLARS OF WESTERN BUDDHISM

DERACINATON, SECULARIZATION, AND INSTRUMENTALIZATION

Barry Magid and Marc R. Poirier

> *Zazen is useless.*
> —"Homeless" Kodo Sawaki

As Buddhist practices have been brought to the West in the decades since World War II, they have undergone a sea change. Both Western converts and Asian teachers of Buddhism, intent on furthering transmission to the West, have adapted the teachings, simplified and altered them, often with the effect of removing meditation practices from their Asian cultural contexts altogether.[1] As a result, a mutually reinforcing dynamic of deracination, secularization, and instrumentalization seems to characterize more and more of Western Buddhism.

The deracination (literally, "cutting off from its roots") of Buddhism is particularly manifested in the removal of meditation practices from their original monastic settings by opening them up to an increasingly lay householder population, with the practices themselves often taught and modeled by lay teachers rather than ordained priests. In the case of the Zen tradition of which we are a part, this transformation can be seen as a continuation of a process of modernization begun in Meiji Japan back before the turn of the twentieth century. Deracination has increasingly secularized Buddhism, sometimes as a deliberate attempt to be responsive to a different cultural milieu. The development of the Western "meditation center," as opposed to the temple or monastery, embodies this ongoing transformation.

What primarily concerns us here is that for its Western followers, along with being secularized, Buddhist practice has been instrumentalized as technique or therapy, whether for the relief of specific symptomatic problems within health care and psychology (anxiety, depression, etc.), or as part of an individual's idiosyncratic program of self-improvement or self-actualization.[2] The problem of instrumentalization can be broadly characterized as locating the value of an activity, not in the activity itself, but exclusively in its outcomes or commodifiable products. It was a central concern of Frankfurt School theorists Horkheimer, Adorno, and Marcuse, as well as, in their own ways, Heidegger, Habermas, and Gadamer. We can only here offer the merest nod of recognition to that extensive body of work, which underlies our concerns.

As we come to more fully understand the dangers and limitations inherent in the instrumentalization of meditation practice, we also see them as the unintended byproducts of secularization and deracination. *The Three Pillars of Zen*, made famous for a generation of students by Philip Kapleau,[3] have traditionally been teaching, practice, and enlightenment. We believe these can no longer be taken for granted to be the foundations of Western Buddhism, given the rapidly changing cultural context in which it's now being transmitted. Though still fundamental to any conception of Zen, Kapleau's pillars are no longer able to bear the weight of the newly constructed edifice of Western Buddhism. In order to accommodate and sustain the incredible influx of lay practitioners, other forces and supports have necessarily been put in place. These new Three Pillars of instrumentalization, secularization, and deracination have enabled the expansion and democratization of Zen, but in doing so, have built a shaky tripod, one which we believe is inherently unstable.

In what follows, we will try to offer an account of a laicized but not secularized Zen practice, one that engages the social and psychological realities of Western life, but which, by not jettisoning its religious core, seeks to avoid the pitfalls of instrumentalized forms of practice. We will attempt to delineate what can allow a practice to remain "religious" in the absence of some of its traditional monastic or temple-based contexts. Further, we will try to tease out the subtleties in distinguishing the processes of secularization (by which Buddhist teachings are made to seem compatible with, or equivalent to, scientific, psychological, or philosophical theories or modes of practice that do not require a commitment to any particular religious community or form of life) and laicization (an extension of Buddhist teachings beyond the traditional renunciant monastic sangha to laypeople and householders, including the trend for teachers, leaders, and officiants of the practice—not only its audience—to consist of laypeople rather than priests).

As Buddhism has become secularized, its teachings have often been offered not as part of a religious, spiritual, or ethical whole, not as a doorway into a rich and complex tradition, but simply as sets of techniques or tools for eliminating some specific source of pain, or for achieving some desired skill or aptitude to better oneself.[4] Mindfulness and meditation techniques are being marketed and increasingly institutionalized as therapy and as personal transformation.[5] The beginner is invited to gain relief from some particular form of suffering—chronic pain, stress, an unskillful relationship, a psychological disorder, a physical illness, stultifying work conditions, poor exam results—or to undertake meditation and mindfulness to acquire happiness or health or workplace success or good relationships or better child-rearing or inner peace[6]: Take this workshop, buy that book or magazine. Sit still for a weekend and be happier. If this one doesn't make you feel better in short order, move on and buy that one. Roshi Pat Enkyo O'Hara calls this approach "mindfulness à la carte."[7] It has also been dubbed "McMindfulness"[8]: quick, effortless, inexpensive, available everywhere, anytime.

All this threatens to obscure the fundamental nature of Buddhism itself. The Zen practices in which we ourselves have been trained have nothing to do with short-term fixes or gains. The experience of awakening passed down from Shakyamuni Buddha entails a radical deconstruction of the very notion of self; it's not a formula for that self to gain increasing mastery over its environment or gain a sense of control or autonomy, let alone achieve calmness or relaxation.

So we offer this chapter as a delineation of the broad difference in two approaches to mindfulness and meditation: the secular, for-gain approach, and what we consider a more genuinely Buddhist no-gain approach. We hold no illusion that what we criticize will be halted or even curtailed as a result of what we write. The shift is too widespread. Materialistic, for-gain Buddhism may well be an unavoidable part of Buddhism's transmission to the West as it adapts to, and is translated into, the deep-rooted individualist, materialist, and secular structures in Western culture—including the culture of science as itself a technique for achieving control and thus better satisfying needs. Obviously, this approach brings gains of its own that we do not mean to dismiss out of hand. Zen Buddhism can and, properly set forth, does address greed, anger, and confusion, but from a totally different angle—by seeing through them, not by eliminating them. So we write about meditation and mindfulness as technique, and we write about Zen not as a technique but ultimately as a religious practice.

We appreciate that most people who investigate and begin a Buddhist practice, such as the one we will describe shortly, are motivated by a desire to fix something painful in their life—loss, illness, inadequacy, shame, some specific psychological distress. Others seek for more than they believe they presently have in their life—understanding, bliss, peace, enlightenment, holiness. But the reasons one begins Buddhist practice must themselves become the object of practice. What I (Magid) have called our "curative fantasies"[9]—the almost inevitable fantasies we all have that practice will make us in some way invulnerable to suffering, free from dependence on unreliable others, or immune to the vicissitudes of change, both in our inner and outer worlds—are almost inevitably concealed within our beginner's mind. These fantasies, of course, fly in the face of the most fundamental of Buddhist principles, interdependence and impermanence. And yet it seems that we all, to one degree or another, psychologically dissociate what we long for practice to achieve from what we all claim to know is the essence of practice.

A sincere and persistent practice of meditation opens the door to appreciating ways in which one contributes to one's own suffering by pushing away the inherent impermanence of life and the fundamental unsatisfactoriness that flows from that truth. Eventually one can begin, perhaps only fleetingly, to understand the self in a different way, as not fixed, but as itself impermanent and interconnected, constantly "realized by the ten thousand things," as Soto Zen Master Dogen wrote.[10]

An ongoing, committed practice of acknowledging life just as it is can have some remarkable results. They are, however, byproducts of practice and not its goals. One traditional list of the perfections, or characteristics of a bodhisattva, include gratitude, clear and virtuous living, patience, energy, concentration, and wisdom.[11] Using more contemporary, psychologically minded language, we might update the list, adding qualities like playfulness, curiosity, and friendliness or loving-kindness. Some clinically proven beneficial results from practice fall within the ambit of some of these larger-scale, traditional fruits of practice. But although the hope of achieving them is why most people come to practice, they in fact occur only after the gradual deconstruction and long-term erosion of self-centered goals.

Taking ancient techniques and focusing them on self-improvement or therapeutic advancement may turn the practice of sustained, quiet exploration and awareness inside out and, in our view, tends to impede and often to defeat it. Practice as gain operates within a familiar frame of separate self, power, and control, in which an "I" seeks to "fix" something, whether "out there" or "deep inside," that is "broken" or "unsatisfactory," or to "gain" something that is currently "missing." Engaging in a traditional Buddhist practice with this underlying frame of mind is unskillful and counterproductive. We call this the "workshop" approach to meditation and mindfulness. Very often, it takes the form of using meditation to induce a particular state of consciousness, which one then hopes to make permanent—a project by definition doomed to failure.

We are aware of a significant irony in our position. That is, we are critical of deracination, secularization, and especially instrumentalization, even as we are in important ways the agents and beneficiaries of these changes. We cannot insulate ourselves from such fundamental trends in modern Buddhism. Moreover, as lay teachers, we ourselves represent a radical break with traditional models of Buddhist practice and transmission. Nonetheless, we wish to sound a cautionary note regarding what we consider to be some unintended and unfortunate consequences of the trends of which we are a part. At the same time, we do not believe that a return to the classic

Asian models, as advocated by some trained in the traditional monastic ways,[12] is a viable alternative for the vast majority of Western practitioners.

WHAT WE TEACH

The most important thing is the practice of awareness, the experiencing of the moment-by-moment manifestation of life-as-it-is. In a formal, regularized way, this should include regular meditation, much as Dogen described it eight hundred years ago, in *Fukanzazengi*.[13] Dogen's description of the actual physical dimension of meditation is simple and straightforward. Just sit down in a quiet place in a comfortable position in which you can be still for some period of time.[14] Place your hands palms up on your lap one on the other, the formal mudra involving the thumb tips touching lightly. Keep your eyes open; stay awake.

Just sitting, shikantaza, is the core of Soto Zen practice.[15] Dogen introduces his presentation of this practice in the *Fukanzazengi* by saying, "This zazen of which I speak is not a technique of meditation but the Dharma gate of joy and ease." In our own teaching, we have attempted to explicate this assertion by saying that a "technique" is a means to an end—and is something that one can do well or badly. Dogen's zazen is meant to be neither of these things. Zazen, for Dogen, is not a means to become enlightened; it is itself the very expression of enlightenment. The very first time a beginner sits down in zazen, he or she has the potential to enter the "Dharma gate of joy and ease." Zazen is the very expression of enlightenment, not a step along the path to enlightenment, not a means to bring about a change of state or consciousness. Zazen is in and of itself the alternative to our usual state of grasping, clinging, and goal-oriented life in general. By sitting down, we have arrived. The scholar T. Griffith Foulk has pointed out[16] that Dogen never uses the word "shikantaza" in his zazen instructions, but he instead uses it only when quoting his own teacher, Rujing, for whom it represented "the dropping off of body and mind." Strictly speaking then, shikantaza should not be used as if it were simply a description of the Soto style of zazen; rather, we should recognize it as the encapsulation of Dogen's expounding of the identity of practice and realization.

Shikantaza, as we understand it and practice it, is full and complete in itself. It is not a technique for self-improvement or change. Practice is a regular and ongoing, nonconceptual expression of the true self, as it is revealed by the myriad experiences of daily life, including those on the cushion. To be sure, a longer-term practitioner is likely to deploy and therefore develop personal qualities such as persistence, energy, faith, constructive doubt, self-discipline, and honesty; but those are not a goal of practice, they happen along the way.

Part of what distinguishes zazen from a meditation "technique" is the religious framework within which it takes place. A zendo, whether in a temple or lay center, is a locus of reverence, ritual, and the marvelous expression of buddha nature in each moment of our practice. It is not a place where we simply engage in spiritual exercises to cultivate this or that state of consciousness. It is not the spiritual equivalent of the gym or health club.

Only when we understand and uphold this frame of reference can we engage in zazen from the noninstrumentalist stance that Dogen recommends. It is from the perspective of the identity of practice and realization that we observe and experience this moment as it is, including the ordinary flow of thought, as it comes and goes. Dogen calls this part "thinking not-thinking," a difficult phrasing that has garnered much commentary but that can, we believe, be simply glossed as this: not the suppression of thoughts, but recognition of the emptiness or insubstantial nature of thought.

My (Magid's) own teacher Charlotte Joko Beck modified the traditional practice by suggesting that distracting thoughts be labeled as part of the process of returning to attention. Labeling means repeating the thought to oneself, "Thinking: when will the bell ring?" Or, when certain thoughts recur over and over, simply stopping and labeling them by category: "pain," "sex," etc. This practice can, if it does not succumb to the temptation of becoming yet another obsessively pursued technique, facilitate awareness of underlying psychological patterns of avoidance, often marked by anxiety or anger, which unconsciously contribute to our evasion of simply being present. These options are meant to help us observe the ways in which we inevitably deviate from the simplicity of zazen into something more like our everyday goal-oriented behaviors. "Just sitting" is so simple we don't know how to do it—or we don't know how to trust something that simple and straightforward. Put another way, we don't know how to trust in the completeness of our minds and our life, just as they are. Our habitual modes of striving and aversion reflexively assimilate meditation, and by attempting to control the uncontrollable, we give rise to and perpetuate the very suffering we mean to hold at bay.

As the founder of her own Ordinary Mind School, Charlotte Joko Beck modified what she had received from her Japanese teacher Maezumi Roshi to explicitly include in her practice instruction a careful attention to psychological patterns and habits. Her writings and talks reflect and model this detailed personal introspection, which we characterize here as paying particular attention to those moments where we deviate from the simplicity of zazen into various avoidant byways. Joko Beck taught that anxiety and anger, in particular, were psychological markers of the boundaries of our willingness to accept the moment just as it is.[17] Greed, anger, delusion, refusal to be with what is: all of these occur everywhere in our everyday lives, and on the cushion as well. The practice of zazen is not an escape from them, but it facilitates a thoroughgoing and ongoing exploration of one's own resistances, attractions, and behaviors. Crucially, however, even our avoidant and "deluded" reactions are themselves simply momentary "dharmas." When seen as such—as empty and transitory—they need not be eliminated or avoided, but they can be simply experienced as they naturally pass by and through our lives. Joko Beck herself insisted that her teaching should not be confused with a form of therapy but as seeing the Absolute in every moment.

Joko Beck was not alone in taking Zen in a psychological direction. It is apparently part of the cultural interpenetration of Zen and other Asian meditation practices with the contemporary Western sensibility, perhaps analogous to the blending of Indian Buddhism with Chinese Taoism that helped give rise to Zen. The move is, in itself, a laicization, secularization, and democratization of Zen practice. In bringing Zen practice close to some styles of psychoanalytic and therapeutic work, it flirts with the instrumentalization of meditation in ways that take it far from Dogen's original vision. Many teachers and authors are engaged in an ongoing exploration of the interface between meditation and psychotherapy.[18] However, the line is easily and often blurred. One should be leery of viewing Zen practice as therapeutic or curative. Opening the ears of one's ears and the eyes of one's eyes (to paraphrase e. e. cummings) makes one more available, in a sense more honest, but doesn't necessarily steer one's life or practice in a particular desired direction.

ON RELIGION

In removing Buddhism from its Asian cultural and religious contexts, many religious aspects of traditional Buddhist practice have been perforce obscured. Laicization, democratization, feminization, and secularization have been and will continue to be consequences of Western converts taking up traditional Asian Buddhist practice. The rise of a generation of fully empowered women teachers, who unlike their Asian counterparts engage in the training of both men and women, in itself is transforming the structures of hierarchy and authority within Western practice centers. At the same time, many Western translations retain and incorporate elements of Eastern practice, either explicitly as part of a religious container, or as some ritualistic elements that may or may not be religious.

The workshop approach attenuates tradition and ritual the most. We think it goes too far, especially the extreme cases where exploration or even mention of the religious roots of the practices are taboo. Even in the self-help/self-improvement workshops that pay lip service to the sources of tradition or incorporate it as part of their "brand," mystery is replaced by the merely mysterious or exotic. Instead of the deep, repetitive ongoing immersion in a complex ritual form that gradually, sometimes only over the course of many years, reveals itself, the workshop goer instead is offered a smorgasbord of chants, texts, and practices that offer the aura of the exotic or of a deracinated mysticism, but without the opportunity to actually engage a single coherent traditional form in any depth. What does it mean to go glibly, seamlessly, weekend to weekend, from African drumming to Tibetan Tantra to a simulacrum of an American Indian sweat lodge? Workshop approaches to mindfulness and meditation are so secular and so deracinated that they can become part of a mix-and-match stew—very much like the New Age approach to spirituality a generation or two ago. Something vital is lost in these creoles. Even within more tradition-minded American Buddhist centers, there is a tendency to offer traditional texts only in translation, so that any engagement with the original language is lost. Accessibility preempts and trumps challenge. Once our "sacred" texts are all in English, there is a temptation to add various inspirational texts from any variety of sources, placing Whitman, Meister Eckhart, and the Song of Songs alongside one another, creating new "lineages" of affinity that both transcend and displace any cultural or historical considerations. There are many valid and compelling reasons to engage in these new synthetic practices—the creation of new women's lineages that acknowledge those forgotten or marginalized by traditional patriarchies is one such example. But we are only beginning to see the unintended consequences of the liberties we are taking.

As we've said, central to the deracination of Western meditation practices is their distancing themselves from their Asian monastic and temple-based forms of life and ritual. Dogen, for instance, taught not only that zazen was the perfect expression of our true nature but that its expression must be extended into every aspect of our daily life, and that the method for this was through the ceremony and ritual of monastic life. Southeast Asian forms of Buddhism, attempting to more closely emulate what they conceive to be the form of life of the Buddha's original sangha, have taught that that very form of life—of poverty, celibacy, homelessness, and lack of any personal attachments or possessions—is the expression of the core truths of impermanence, nonclinging, and interdependency. In none of these traditions was meditation separable either from an all-encompassing form of life or from a strict ethical set of precepts governing all aspects of conduct.[19]

Prefiguring some of the later Western cultural upheavals, the Japanese Meiji-era edict that temple priests could marry radically transformed and upset the traditional paradigm in the eyes of many Asian Buddhists, for whom celibacy and the priesthood were and are synonymous. That true realization could take place outside of monastic orders was always considered something of an anomaly, and the examples of enlightened lay-people were considered rare and noteworthy. All of this has been upended yet further in Western Buddhism, in particular by the secularized mindfulness movement. Meditation as a "technique" no longer requires any familiarity, let alone commitment to, Buddhism as a religious practice or form of life. The practice of meditation by laypeople is no longer considered a watered-down or popularized version of "the real thing"—which is practiced in monasteries—and commitment to practice no longer culminates in ordination or the taking of monastic vows. As lay teachers we are part of this shift.

It is only in this newly secularized context that the question can arise whether Buddhist teaching is necessarily to be headed up by priests or monks. Part of the laicization process has been the emergence of lay teachers for the growing audience of lay students, teachers who are themselves authorized to authorize the next generation of lay teachers. The generation of Americans (notably Goldstein, Kornfield, Salzberg, et al.) who studied in Southeast Asia and, rather than becoming monks themselves, became teachers of mindfulness and insight meditation, explicitly recast a monastic practice into a secular form for nonrenunciant householders. American and other Western Zen teachers of all lineages have, with increasing frequency, authorized lay teachers, who operate outside of priestly ritual and hierarchy. Thus, in the United States we have a Lay Zen Teachers Association (LZTA) comprised of lay teachers and of a few members who are in fact ordained but who hold themselves out as lay teachers rather than relying on priesthood for their authority. This group works to share their experimentation with the form, within a context that is familiar with and often incorporates the religious elements from Asian Buddhism. Lay teaching demystifies Zen practice, but it does not abandon its religious aspect. LZTA coexists with two other organizations in the United States: the American Zen Teachers Association (AZTA), comprised increasingly of both priests and lay teachers, and the Soto Zen Teachers Association (SZTA), which insists on ordination in a form prescribed by the central Soto institution in Japan and which maintains the inseparability of ordination and Dharma transmission. In our view, there is a legitimate role for the priestly function as celebrant of life events—births, marriages, deaths—but priesthood is not necessary to the teaching of Zen nor to the perpetuation of a religious tradition. Historically there are a few traditional examples of lay Zen practitioners of the highest order. The Sixth Zen Patriarch, Huineng, was one. Quaker practice provides a familiar and contemporary example of a Christian religious tradition that is rigorously horizontal and nonpriestly and that has persisted for hundreds of years. While it would not surprise us if some of the manifestation of Western lay Zen teaching eventually took on forms similar to those of the Quakers, the unique role of the teacher in Zen would seem to require the preservation of some degree of teaching authority and hierarchy.

Zen practice is religious in another sense that is important to describe. Because the sustained practice of just sitting opens, softens, and embraces life as it is, it has a quality of tying into the interconnectedness of being. It provides a regular, ritualized context for engaging impermanence. We would not want to say that there is a goal within practice of experiencing, from time to time, in meditation, a moment-by-moment quality that is "eternal, selfless, joyful, and pure."[20] That would turn practice into a kind of thirsty mysticism, when it is in fact working toward direct encounter. But that sort of experience does happen. The process of showing up, slowing down, stepping back, and settling in, is, in our view, religious in an important sense: grounded in appreciation and reverence for life as it is and in a compassionate response to the suffering of the world. There is nothing in that definition that explicitly requires the mediation of a priesthood. It is simply a matter of what forms of life evolve in a particular historical and cultural context to enable individuals to engage in practice.

Religion is, however, not part of the vocabulary in much workshop-style teaching. We've seen and talked with instructors in secular settings who seemed perfectly aware of a religious aspect of practice. It may even have been the foundation of their training. But there are constraints, imposed within secular settings, for the teaching itself to be secular and nondenominational. One can see the legitimate need for avoiding anything that appears to be proselytizing of a particular religious faith within corporate or educational settings. But it is also part of the secular, market-based pitch that mindfulness is a technique that can be separated from any long-term commitments, lifestyle changes, or ethical concerns. There is something wrong when teachers of mindfulness and meditation who are informed by Buddhist practice feel that they cannot share that with those they are teaching. Their teaching becomes narrow and subtly imbued with shame or fear. Things will only get worse if, as we suspect, the Buddhist roots of mindfulness and meditation are deliberately expunged by corporate clients, as we understand may happen with the Google product, for example.

The designation of a practice as religious furthermore describes a level of lifelong commitment, both to the practice itself and to the community in which it is embedded. For the notion of sangha to be viable, we must have a group of practitioners who are committed to one another, not just to their own meditation practice. They must be united by something more substantial than the coincidence of meeting up at irregular intervals at a smorgasbord of workshops. This commitment is not merely a matter of peer support but of a shared ethical responsibility, based on the precepts. Further, our Western psychodynamic understanding of attachment leads us to place great value on a long-term relationship with the teacher. We do not believe that teachers are fungible, interchangeable vessels for conveying the Dharma. Working through our own self-centered versions of attachment requires that we engage the transferential permutations of idealization, identification, and dependency within the context of a long-term trustworthy relationship with our teacher. Intermittent contact and repeatedly switching from one teacher to another, or one tradition to another, runs the danger of keeping students perpetual beginners. Rather than deepen their practice over a lifetime, they are liable to have a beginner's first-year experience over and over and over.

It is fashionable in many circles these days to ask regarding some new technique or innovation, "Is it scalable?" Can something that works for ten people, or twenty or thirty, be made to work equally well for a hundred, a thousand, or ten thousand? We can think of the mindfulness movement as an attempt to make meditation scalable: available and accessible in numbers never possible in a traditional monastic model of practice. We trust that it is obvious that something is both gained and lost in this effort, perhaps in a way analogous to offering a patient ten sessions of cognitive behavioral therapy instead of ten years of psychoanalysis. The relative merits of these alternatives are not measurable by outcome studies. Thinking in terms of measurable outcomes, rather than the felt experience of a long-term immersion in a process of self-inquiry and self-discovery, is itself a byproduct of a short-term approach.

The Middle Way has deep ditches on each side of the path. We do not believe Buddhism in America can flourish either by attempting to recreate Asian monastic forms or by making simple, therapeutically oriented techniques of mindfulness available to the public through a hodgepodge of classes, workshops, and self-help manuals. We see ourselves as attempting to find our way in uncharted territory where the role of teachers and the very nature of practice and practice settings are already being transformed by the intersecting processes of secularization, laicization, and instrumentalization. All of these combine to make possible our experimental alternatives to Asian monasticism, and all of these may equally combine to make shaky and uncertain the foundations of our new forms of practice. We do not pretend to have a solution to this dilemma, nor do we assume the coming of the Dharma to the West is preordained to success. The scandals that rocked the first generation of Buddhist communities were not unfortunate anomalies, but rather they were symptomatic of a widespread disconnect between American fantasies and idealizations of liberation and enlightenment, and the reality that Asian forms of practice did little to work through, at a psychological level, the shadow side of teachers and students alike.

What the way forward will be we do not know. Our attempt here is simply to throw some light on the ditches that line the path and offer a warning to tread slowly and carefully.

4. MINDFULNESS MYTHS

FANTASIES AND FACTS

Robert Meikyo Rosenbaum

To present mindfulness as a Western technique extracted from its Asian religious and spiritual context, proponents want to demonstrate that it is both verifiable and useful. This kind of empirical approach can be informative and very much in keeping with the pragmatic spirit of Buddhist inquiry. On the other hand, approaching mindfulness as if it is a thing that can be grasped, taken out for examination, evaluated, and judged for its usefulness is inherently antithetical to what Zen sometimes calls "Big Mind" or "Mirror Mind."

Mind with a capital "M" is, for Zen, the ground of being. Mirror Mind is all-accepting because it does not discriminate good or bad, big or little; it simply reflects whatever comes. It does not strive to accomplish any particular goal or serve as a means to a utilitarian end. Some of its flavor can be intuited from a title of a book by Zen teacher Robert Aitken: *The Mind of Clover.*

The importance of this Mind is not restricted to Zen: it is omnipresent in all traditional mindfulness practices, which cultivate nonjudging, openness, nonattachment, and acceptance to promote clear seeing that goes beyond self-centered striving. The *Tao Te Ching*, which predated both Zen and Vipassana and had a strong influence on both, puts it this way in verse 67:

The whole world says my Way is great.
Great but useless.
Because it is great, it has no use.
If it were useful,
It would long have been small.[1]

Along these lines, when I was discussing the topic of outcome research on mindfulness, my coeditor Barry Magid said, "Once one begins to discuss 'outcomes' you are already wrong."

Nevertheless, a large number of well-intentioned practitioners and students of meditation are using research methods as part of their path of inquiry. Many of them do so with full awareness of the caveats and limitations involved; the problem arises when these cautions and qualifications are ignored and oversimplified. This sort of inquiry is quite different from the kind of basic scientific research that feels it is most successful not when it "proves" something we want to find out but when it raises interesting new questions. Demonstrating something "works" is a very modern, and especially a very American, concern. As Poirier noted in his chapter in this book, the rhetoric of science can be insidious, employed by marketers seeking to exploit a model of meditation for gain, rather than for open-minded exploration.

Everything is being subjected these days to outcome analysis. Unfortunately, most outcome measures and satisfaction surveys are so poorly constructed they do not provide reliable or valid information.[2] But they give the illusion that they do, and thus they provide reassurance to our ever-present worry that we are gullible marks being sold a bill of goods (a constant worry in a consumerist society where everything is turned into commodities) and that what we are doing might not be "worth it" (again, note the consumerist concern with relative value).

It's nice to have evidence to help you believe in what you're doing. But perhaps we should recall a cautionary tale:

In ages past, as people began to meditate, the followers of Mara (the king of deception) became concerned. They said to Mara: "What happens if these people start to get an inkling of the truth?"

Mara replied: "Don't worry. These humans—as soon as they get a glimpse of the truth, they make a belief out of it."[3]

Beliefs are powerful. People will kill for them. People will die for them. We bolster our beliefs with scraps of evidence—and when the need is great enough and the conviction fervent enough, we usually can find some. So we need to be careful not to let our desire to help people practice mindfulness lead to our accepting scientific evidence uncritically, in order to use it as a cudgel to convince.

A lot of Zen practice is about letting go of our beliefs, so we don't get caught clinging to hoped-for outcomes or cherished systems of thoughts and feelings. Instead, Zen relies on great faith: plunging wholeheartedly in to a practice, no matter where it might lead or what kind of experience ensues. Buddhist mindfulness practices were originally skillful means to help people to discover there is nothing at all we can hold to.

How does this play out when we evaluate mindfulness practice according to its practical utility? I will not attempt to evaluate the thousands of studies on mindfulness, of which I have only read several hundred. There are meta-analyses and reviews available that do that. Instead, I will focus on some of the questionable conceptual underpinnings that come into play in much of the research, citing specific studies only for illustrative purposes. For example, I find it somewhat ironic that mindfulness teachers—who stress the evanescence of thought and the impermanence of feelings, perceptions, formations, and consciousness—often grasp a bit too firmly at the published studies that enable them to enthuse about brain research.

BUT WE KNOW MINDFULNESS PRACTICE
CHANGES THE BRAIN!

Well, yes. Meditation (of any sort) does change the brain. But *everything* we do changes the brain. If you close your eyes, your EEG changes. If, while lying in an MRI brain scan, you breathe deeply, the movement artifacts make for an unclear image; the same is true if you tap your fingers during the scan. For a clear brain scan, you must lie perfectly still in a claustrophobic chamber while magnets thunk and clang around you. It's not clear how well what is measured there (changes in brain oxygenation, patterns of blood flow) generalizes to everyday experience.

It's true that if you practice meditation, brain scans are likely to show structural changes in the brain over time. The same is true if you practice the piano (according to studies, musicians show more bilateral brain activity than nonmusicians), or if you work for thirty years as a bricklayer (one otherwise demented patient I saw had preserved "right-hemisphere" spatial abilities from his many years of making bricks fit a predetermined layout in his construction job). I suspect if you were to spend eight hours a day in front of the TV doing nothing but watching reruns of *Star Trek*, we'd see some interesting changes in the white matter of your brain.

The fact is, noninvasive brain measures are still very blunt tools. Brain scans and EEGs cannot, by themselves, diagnose Alzheimer's disease or seizure disorders. Part of the problem is that research usually reports findings in terms of the *average* patient: the range of normal individual variation is so large that these "average" findings don't help much in assessing a particular individual.

An older adult can have a brain scan that is full of spots and atrophy but can show no sign of dementia; the reverse is also true. If brain scans and medical tests cannot reliably detect the effects of seizures in the brain unless they actually observe them while they're happening, if they can't diagnose the heartbreaking diseases of dementia, is it reasonable to expect brain measures to tell us much about the subtle differences in brain states that occur from meditation?

(A related fact: on average, there are differences between male and female brains, but the range of *intra*-gender variation is greater than the range of *inter*-gender variation. A similar finding seems likely if we start to compare people within and between different meditation traditions: we might find more differences between individuals than between techniques of meditation.)

Brain measures can be effective adjuncts to a diagnostic workup, but neurologists and neuropsychologists still must make most diagnoses by examining how somebody actually functions in daily life, in both structured and unstructured situations. Often it's the people closest to a patient who provide the crucial information for a diagnosis, telling us what we cannot observe in an examination room and what the patient might not be aware of him- or herself. The same might be said about meditation: instead of relying on magnetic imaging and radioactive isotopes to tell us meditation is "working" for a person, wouldn't it be better to assess the effects of meditation on individuals by finding out if they treat the people and objects around them with more kindness and compassion?

There's also a basic fallacy in thinking that because a part of the brain lights up during a brain scan, that's the part responsible for a particular mental state. Yes, there's lots of evidence that meditation results in changes in, say, the frontal lobes ("associated with self-regulation"). But it's unlikely meditation is restricted to the frontal lobes, which in any case are massively connected to all the other parts of the brain. In fact, it's questionable *any* cognitive activity can be isolated in one small part of the brain, despite what you may read in the mass media. There are substantial methodological difficulties in localization research, whose usual technique measures overall, ongoing brain function and then subtracts it from what is seen when the brain is performing a particular task. If in real life you "subtracted" that resting activity from the brain, the person would be dead.

To give an example of how localization can lead us astray: we've known for a century that the "auditory cortex" processes sound and the "visual cortex" processes sight. Recent research, though, has discovered the *visual* information we receive from another person's lips during a conversation is processed by the *auditory* cortex.[4] The trend in neuroscience is to see the brain as not divided into neat little isolated sections, but functioning according to complex distributed networks.

It also is worth heeding the caution of Rafael Yuste and George Church, two prominent neuroscientists involved in the cutting-edge Brain Activity Map Project:

The media routinely report on scans showing that specific brain locations light up when we feel [X or Y]... these news stories may give the impression that current technology provides fundamental insights into how the brain works, but that impression is deceiving... We are still *completely ignorant* [my italics] of how... to bridge the gap between the firing of neurons and cognition, perception, emotion.[5]

Meditation is a flower of the mind. The mind is not the brain. The mind relies on the brain, but together with the brain it also relies on and reflects the heart, lungs, liver, kidneys; the bacteria in the gut; the chlorophyll that converts energy from the sun; the water and the air and the efforts of all the myriad beings. Simultaneously each and all of these rely on and reflect the mind.

The human brain weighs about three pounds, is about the size of two fists, and has about 85 billion neurons. But however much our ideas and desires may weigh on us, the mind itself weighs nothing; however big or small our sense of ourselves, the mind is vast beyond measurement; however many thoughts and feelings we have, the activities of the mind are innumerable even while its stillness is unbreakable.

Relying on neuroscience to validate Dharma practice implies that the spiritual practice of meditation is not valuable in and of itself: we must justify it with something outside itself. In principle, neuroscience does not constitute a privileged position as the external standard of validation: why not measure whether meditation changes muscle strength or, for that matter, whether it makes your fingernails less subject to splitting and breaking? The reader might protest: "But meditation is something you do with your brain, not your muscles or fingernails." This is not correct. We do not meditate with our brain: we meditate with our whole body and mind. When Bodhidharma, who is credited with bringing Zen meditation practice to China, interviewed his successors in a famous dialog and bequeathed his heritage to them, he gave them his skin, flesh, bone, and marrow: the brain was not mentioned.

We are currently beguiled by the brain and by our new brain-scanning technology, but even from a strictly anatomical perspective it is a mistake to treat the brain in isolation from the rest of the nervous system: the brain extends into the spine and has both afferent and efferent connections through the peripheral nerves—not to mention the emerging findings that suggest gut bacteria alter the levels of neurotransmitters in the brain. Also let us not forget that Asian calligraphy uses a single character to depict mind and *heart* as an inseparable unity: where the brain fits in this realm is not necessarily so clear.

The Western need to justify a practice by measuring and quantifying assumes utilitarianism as the highest good, but this is ultimately tragic, for it implies you, too, must justify yourself as having some use. Simply being yourself, it seems, is somehow not enough.

So the next time you see a report that an intervention has resulted in changes in the dorsal striatum, left anterior insula, and the orbitofrontal cortex—all commonly associated with increased well-being and self-regulation in the brain-and-meditation research—you might want to remember one research report where this finding did not come from a study of meditation. Instead, they were found after a single twenty-minute exposure to UV rays in a tanning salon.[6]

MAKES TEETH WHITER—
PROVEN EFFECTIVE IN CLINICAL TRIALS!

One of the reasons mindfulness practices have become so popular is because research seems to demonstrate their effectiveness. There is a great deal of excitement about the evidence that mindfulness is useful in clinical settings, suggesting mindfulness can be a natural partner to psychology for making mental disciplines "scientific." A careful examination of the research, though, reveals how enthusiastic proselytizing can sometimes be less than mindful of the complexities and caveats involved.

It sometimes seems as if mindfulness advocates claim that their practice is the first and foremost method of meditation to receive scientific validation. This is not the case. Research in the 1960s and 1970s on Transcendental Meditation, the Benson Relaxation Response, and other practices such as yoga, the Quieting Reflex, etc., reported strong effects on physical and psychological health. In those years there was a growing interest in the effects of stress on immune function, health, and well-being—which continues to this day. Benson's research, in particular, dates back to the 1960s and is supported by many studies of its power to benefit patients with cardiovascular disease.[7] In fact, the benefits of quiet, relaxation, and stress management are so powerful it is often difficult to demonstrate that meditation contributes much beyond potentiating and enhancing the non-specific mechanisms at play in deep relaxation.

This issue is exacerbated by the fact that the mindfulness-based approaches examined in much of the research are "packages" containing a number of elements. The excellent program of Mindfulness-Based Stress Reduction (MBSR, initiated by Jon Kabat-Zinn at the Center for Mindfulness in Medicine, which helped jump-start the boom in mindfulness) includes, in addition to mindfulness meditation, didactic instruction, elements of cognitive therapy, yoga, and group process. It can be hard to separate out the effective ingredients in MBSR or in related programs.

The variety of mindfulness programs highlights another problem: people differ in how they conceptualize mindfulness, and it has come to have such a wide variety of connotations its meaning is increasingly muddy.[8] Mindfulness researchers also differ in how they operationalize mindfulness, the length of training they provide, the kinds of control and comparison groups they employ, and what kind of measurements they use.[9]

But regardless of other variables, all the research on mindfulness interventions face the same difficulty: how do you measure mindfulness? Usually this is done via self-report questionnaires, but there are a multitude of different questionnaires in use[10] and they do not always agree with each other. As always with such questionnaires, reasonable questions can be raised as to how accurate participants' self-reports can be—especially when you are talking about something as complex as observing the efficacy with which you observe yourself.

The limits of self-report measures are illustrated in an excellent paper by Willoughby Britton and her colleagues in a study of the effects of mindfulness meditation on sleep problems.[11] They found people with sleep problems who went through an eight-week mindfulness-based cognitive therapy program reported, at the end of the program, that they were sleeping better. However, they had not improved any more than had people in a waiting-list control group. In fact, once they measured actual sleep with polysomnography in a sleep lab, the meditators actually showed increased wakefulness and *decreased* sleep propensity—indicating that meditators' self-report did not match up with objective measures. Britton comments there is a popular belief that meditation helps sleep, apparently supported by prior research that used only self-report measures. Some research is better than others, and sometimes popular enthusiasm can outpace the scientific research.

To the extent that mindfulness can be developed as a skill, we would expect the level of the skill to vary from time to time and in different situations. Questionnaire measures give global mindfulness ratings that may not reflect important differences in what happens in specific circumstances. Would the man who filled out a questionnaire rating himself high on mindfulness immediately before or after a class in MBSR fill out the questionnaire the same way an hour later at home—especially if someone ran into his car on the way back? In general, questionnaires that assess transient *states* are less valid the more time there is between performing the activity and the administration of the questionnaire. On the other hand, if mindfulness is conceived as a *trait* rather than an activity, how do stable traits fit in with a practice that emphasizes the continuous shifts of transient inner experiences? Furthermore, the questionnaire measures rarely tap into the subtle aspects of the qualitative experience of meditation, with its self-recursiveness: for example, in the common mindfulness exercise of noticing when one is judging a thought or a feeling, it can be difficult to notice whether you are judging the act of judging.

The growth in mindfulness research studies is impressive. Up until 1999, there were fewer than fifteen studies published each year. By 2013 there were more than five hundred studies in that single year.[12] The studies seem to convince by their sheer number, and I have heard many teachers in mindfulness programs say "research supports us."

But quantity does not equate with—indeed, it can obscure—clarity. For example, a recent meta-analysis of mindfulness-based therapy started with an initial pool of 727 studies; about half of the studies had to be excluded because they were not quantitative, or were simply descriptive case reports. An additional substantial number were then excluded because they either didn't include a clearly specified form of mindfulness, provided insufficient data, or used poor measures. Eventually, the authors of the meta-analysis determined only 39 of the initial 727 studies were suitable for further examination.[13]

The gold standard in outcome research is random assignment to double-blind groups. Without double-blinding, there is always a strong likelihood that expectancy effects (on the part of both program leaders and participants) will affect the results. Unfortunately, it's virtually impossible to achieve a double-blind condition for mindfulness programs—a study in which neither the subject nor the researcher would know whether mindfulness was being taught and practiced. However, at least it is possible to provide random assignment (i.e., enroll participants in different programs according to a roll of the dice, even though both participants and program leaders know which one they're in), and there have been summary reviews and meta-analyses of mindfulness in such trials.[14]

In general, the authors of the summary studies (who usually are sympathetic to mindfulness) conclude that mindfulness programs are helpful. However, independent reviewers usually offer more cautions. For example, while Bassam Khoury and his colleauges conclude from their meta-analysis that mindfulness-based therapy is moderately to largely effective for a variety of psychological problems,[15] the University of York's Centre for Reviews and Dissemination comments, "The authors' conclusions may be overstated given the poor quality and wide variation between studies."[16]

When I examined the Khoury meta-analysis more closely, I found an interesting pattern, one that seems to hold for many reviews. The overall conclusion initially seems to be that mindfulness-based therapy is "moderately effective." However, this was true mostly for studies that consisted of comparisons between pretreatment and posttreatment participants or in comparisons between people who received mindfulness "treatment" and waiting-list controls. Here the effect size was moderate: a respectable (if not overwhelming) 0.55.[17] However, when mindfulness-based therapy was compared to other active treatments (supportive therapy, art therapy, relaxation, psychoeducation) the effect size shrank markedly to 0.33; when mindfulness-based therapy was compared to psychotherapy, the effect size shrank to a range between 0.13 and 0.22, which is considered quite small.

Similarly in Keng, Smoski, and Robins's review of empirical studies of the effects of mindfulness on psychological health, the sheer quantity of the data leads to an impression of superior effectiveness for mindfulness. A careful examination of the tables listing the results of the 56 studies they review, however, shows that the mindfulness intervention is actually superior to the comparison intervention in only about two-thirds of the studies: a majority of instances, to be sure, but hardly an overwhelming finding, given the probable effects of experimenter bias (since neither participants nor instructors were blind to what was being studied), and the fact that the mindfulness meditations were always mixed in with other interventions (group therapy, dialectical behavioral therapy, psychoeducation, etc.). One cannot be sure how much mindfulness meditation itself was at the root of the improvements.[18]

In short the research is encouraging but not definitive. Please note I am not saying mindfulness is not effective. I have no doubt that mindfulness programs have benefitted many, many people. However, I am somewhat skeptical that mindfulness is remarkably *more* effective than other meditations or, in clinical settings, other treatment options. The danger is that overpreaching its benefits may cause a backlash when the reality comes up against the hype, and disappointed clients (both institutional and individual) will turn against not only mindfulness programs but all meditations and complementary approaches.

It's not surprising, after all, that mindfulness-based interventions help people. Most interventions delivered by a caring teacher, therapist, or coach to a motivated person in need will help. But the current research's focus on establishing an overgeneralized effectiveness leaves us without good data to help us determine more specific intervention strategies: which kind of meditation (or other therapeutic approach) is best for what kind of person dealing with which kind of problem.

WHAT MINDFULNESS RESEARCH MISSES: PSYCHOLOGICAL SCIENCE AND MINDFULNESS

Studies on the efficacy of mindfulness in clinical contexts represent a type of investigation very familiar to psychotherapy researchers: "Is technique

A (e.g., cognitive-behavioral therapy) superior to technique B (e.g., psychodynamic psychotherapy) or method C (e.g., medication)?" After sixty years, huge effort and expense, and thousands of pages of journal articles, it's become clear this is, if not exactly the wrong question, something that distracts us from more important issues.

Psychotherapy research has found, when it comes to clinical outcomes, client factors such as motivation, general level of psychological health, socioeconomic status, etc., are far more important than techniques. Techniques account for at most 15% of the outcome variance according to Lambert's frequently cited estimate,[19] and perhaps as little as 2% of the variance according to Wampold's review.[20] In contrast, client factors and extratherapeutic factors (events in the client's life) account for between 40% to 87% of the outcome. After these client factors, it is the relationship between client and therapist that matters most, contributing about a third of the variance in outcome.[21]

The finding that it is the client, not the therapist nor the technique, that is most important in the process of change is not a popular finding among adherents for this or that particular "brand" of treatment, but the evidence is overwhelming. It's also completely consistent with traditional Buddhism, in which the techniques available are regarded as skillful means to help a person on the Path, but ultimately it is the person's own practice that's crucial. (This is alongside "causes and conditions," which can refer to karma, the effects of past actions, people's current life situation, whether they encounter the Dharma, and so forth. These would play a role roughly equivalent to that of "extratherapeutic factors" in psychotherapy.) There are many excellent teachers of mindfulness who are well aware of the importance of these client and relationship factors, but the research on mindfulness tends to direct our attention to the technique rather than to the person, to the method rather than the practice journey, to the manualized curriculum rather than the relationship between the student and the teacher.

Since the beginning of the twentieth century, the time of the Freudians and the early behaviorists, there has been controversy about the role of "conscious" versus "unconscious" mental activity. At the moment, the pendulum has swung to the cognitive-behaviorists, who preach a gospel that we have fairly easy access to our mental processes. By observing our thoughts, they say, we can identify "irrational distortions" that warp our feelings.

This is undeniably very useful clinically, but a vast body of research indicates there are limits to conscious awareness. A consensus is emerging that there are a variety of mental processes; some of which (using Daniel Kahneman's terminology[22]) are fast and kick in automatically without our awareness, others of which are relatively slow but, when employed with intentional conscious control, can override the faster automatic processes; and still others that have effects completely out of our control and awareness.

For example, subtle social cues affect our behavior. One experiment in an office that had an honor system to fund the coffee and tea found that the amount of money donated was less if the poster behind the coffee pot had a neutral landscape than when the poster contained a person looking out toward the coffee drinker. People never noticed the poster, but their money talked for them.

There is a significant body of research on cognitive biases, which usually operate not so much *without* as *despite* our awareness. One of the most dramatic is the "continuation bias." Put simply, if we do something often, we tend to keep doing it even in situations where it is clearly inappropriate. This can be observed when pilots crash-land: black box tapes show the pilots are frequently aware that something is wrong (visibility is poor, instruments are acting oddly, etc.), and they actively consider aborting the landing, but they decide to go ahead in spite of the contrary evidence. The landing sequence is a habit reinforced by multiple successful landings: "It's always worked before."

Mindfulness does not necessarily protect us against such fatalities. We all can get into a rut. In fact, in some ways meditation promotes certain kinds of beneficial ruts. This can lead meditation communities (whether they be religious or secular organizations) to adhere to practices that not only don't work but not infrequently have led to abuse and harm. For this reason, it might behoove all of us who devote ourselves to a meditation practice to not expect meditation to cure all our ills, but to also incorporate some of what we've learned about the vagaries of human behavior—our unconscious processes and cognitive biases—from psychological science.

Mindfulness may give us the impression that if we are sufficiently conscious and attentive we will be able to achieve what we want, whether it be cultivating kindness, making ourselves immune to stress, or succeeding in a business venture. As noted above, automatic "fast" cognitive processes and habitual biases show us there are significant limitations: neither attention nor consciousness can rule all our actions. In addition, we run into problems when we conflate mindfulness with just paying attention.

Too often we say "I tripped over that because I wasn't mindful" when we mean "I tripped over that because I wasn't paying attention." Attention is a very complex phenomenon. Neuropsychological models of attention often distinguish between its components: basic level of alertness; ability to take in information accurately; ability to sustain *and* to shift attention as needed.[23] Another way of looking at attention is to think of it as a kind of beam of light that can be narrow or wide, scanning or fixed on one point; it can also be brighter or dimmer, sharply focused or blurred.[24]

Traditional meditation trainings vary in regard to which kinds of attention they develop: subsuming all sorts of attention under the general rubric of "mindfulness" can obscure the need to apply certain kinds of attention in some situations and not others. Perhaps what modern psychology and neuroscience are learning about attention might help supplement the categories of consciousness expounded in Buddhism[25] and help us develop novel meditations that can supplement the traditional ones. Still, no matter how developed our powers of attention may be, nobody can be attentive to everything all the time. You'd be overwhelmed by the flood of information and unable to function.

Perhaps the greatest contribution of psychology over the last hundred years has been how its findings offer an opportunity to develop a deep sense of genuine humility. Just as the Copernican revolution dethroned humanity from the center of the cosmos, so the findings of psychology have taught us we are not in full control of our minds; this "I" we each cherish as "me" is not necessarily at the center of our actions. A huge amount of our behavior is automatic.[26] We are subject to the limitations of attention, to the frailties of our cognitive biases, of our habits, and of emotional currents we are not even usually aware of.

These findings are quite consistent with the central Buddhist insight that all being is inter-being. "I" cannot exist alone, and the idea that meditation will make me into an "I" who, completely "mindful," is self-sufficient, happily in charge of the world within and the world around me, is a fantasy. A related fantasy—one all too common among well-meaning meditation practitioners—is that we will be able to improve our practice by simply employing right intentions and enough willpower. This brings the ego back into the center of the picture.

Something like this is, I think, at work in the way people view research on mindfulness. Paradoxically, the "hard science" of research swallowed uncritically makes us more credulous: it enhances the fantasy that meditation is somehow magical, that by meditating we will not have to confront the hard work of placing our difficulties within the context of how we are living our lives and the messy specifics of how to change our behaviors.

The fact is, we are all human. We are attached to our habitual ways of doing things—even when they don't work well. Meditation practice can help us gain some freedom from aversion and attachment, but the basic mechanism of gravitating toward pleasure and away from pain is so hard-wired into all living organisms it's unreasonable to expect mindfulness (or any meditation or psychological technique) to make us immune from it. In the religious sphere, meditation can tempt us with the fantasy that we can be more than human, some kind of super-being, if we only attain *anuttara samyak sambodhi*, supreme perfect enlightenment. In the secular sphere, meditation can tempt us with the fantasy that we can control our thoughts and feelings and achieve superproductivity and happiness just through our personal efforts.

But we're all fallible, and we're all in this together. This is why being part of a community is part of traditional meditation practice; it helps to have other people around to point out your blind spots. Doing "mindfulness meditation" in isolation is like doing an isometric exercise in the gym or rehearsing scenarios in video games as preparation for, say, playing a good game of baseball; it might help, but it's not the best way to practice. Similarly, attending a time-limited group program in mindfulness is different from being in an ongoing practice community for decades. We might be able to assess the effects of mindfulness meditation on symptom reduction, but ultimately the test of the wide realm of Buddhist practice is how you face your life and face your death. The former is difficult to quantify, and it's very difficult to do a self-report outcome assessment of the latter.

Solitary gym work and animated simulations can be helpful and fun, but ultimately there's no substitute for real practice in the actual setting. When you get out on the field and deal with whatever comes at you, you find out if you can handle a routine grounder or hit a wicked curve. In examining the effects of meditation, we should not rely too much on the chambers of brain scans and the charts of clinical studies. They have their place, but ultimately we need to practice with what's right in front of us.

Shorn of evidence, shorn of belief, how do you find your place right where you are?

5. ONE BODY, WHOLE LIFE

MINDFULNESS AND ZEN

Hozan Alan Senauke

When I was ordained at Berkeley Zen Center nearly thirty years ago I received a lineage document common to our Soto Zen Buddhist tradition. The document is a vertical list of Indian, Chinese, Japanese, and Western ancestors, running from Shakyamuni Buddha to my teacher, Hakuryu Sojun, with my new Buddhist name, Hozan Kushiki, written at the bottom of the list. Below that is a text containing the following language:

> The preceptual vein of the Buddha is the one-great-causal-condition of our lineage gate, personally passed from Buddha on Gridhakuta Peak... Protect and hold these precepts. Do not let them be cut off.[1]

In the years since, I have studied the precepts as they occur historically and currently in the various Buddhist traditions. The most common version directs practitioners not to kill, not to steal, not to lie, not to misuse sexuality, and not to indulge in intoxicants—"rules" shared by many systems of morality. In his creative and expansive interpretation of the precepts, Vietnamese Zen Master Thich Nhat Hanh calls these the Five Mindfulness Trainings.[2] In other words, there is a direct connection between morality and mindfulness, and it is a connection cultivated by training or continuous reinforcement. They share a home in the middle of the Eightfold Path; this is the "preceptual vein of the Buddha" we vow to uphold.

The Pali word *sati* is not fully encompassed by the English "mindfulness," Thomas Rhys Davids's late nineteenth-century translation. *Sati*, or the Sanskrit *smrti*, can be translated as "remembering" or "recollection." One remembers oneself and one's intention moment by moment. One takes the scattered pieces of actions or awareness and re-collects them in wholeness.

The Japanese character for mindfulness is *nen*, which is written as a character that has two parts—念 . The top part means *ima* or "now"; the base is *shin* or "heart/mind." So one can see *nen* as both the mind-moment itself, manifesting in thought after thought, and as the momentary-now-*awareness* of a thought. In each mind-moment one attends to the ceaseless rising and falling away of each feeling, sensation, or thought, and in its entirety mindfulness cultivates a continuity of awareness that weaves all activities into whole cloth.

Zen, as handed down by generations of teachers, applies this to a whole-life practice. Life in a Zen temple, monastery, or retreat includes work practice, cooking and eating, study, bathing, and rest. There is an emphasis on upright, seated meditation, but Zen is fundamentally a one-body practice. The community sits, eats, and works together. Walking meditation is done slowly, in a long circular line, walking in pace with each other. Young monks in training sleep side-by-side in the meditation hall, each with a single three-by-six-foot mat as a living space. Several Zen monasteries in the West carefully preserve the precise forms of this tradition, and even our mostly lay Zen centers and communities keep to the spirit of the practice, helping students train in a way that allows this spirit to pervade one's daily activities, including work and family life.

This Zen emphasis on one-body, whole-life practice raises some interesting questions about the nature of mindfulness. The Buddha's comprehensive instruction on Right Mindfulness is found in the Satipatthana Sutta,[3] the "Foundations of Mindfulness." Succinctly, the first three foundations of mindfulness involve observing body and mind: (1) awareness of one's body, including breath; (2) awareness of feelings at the most basic level of perception: pleasant, unpleasant, and neutral; (3) awareness of one's mind: thoughts, emotions, stories, the flow of consciousness. The fourth foundation, mindfulness of the dharmas, involves looking at mind and body through various lenses of Buddhist analysis or psychological systems.

While these traditional practices date to the Buddha's earliest teachings, they are frequently found in the later Mahayana texts. The thirteenth-century Zen master Dogen, in his poetic way, speaks of mindfulness in *Shobogenzo Sanjushichihon Bodai Bumpo (On the Thirty-Seven Methods of Training for Realizing Enlightenment)*:

> "The root of mindfulness" is the circle of those withered trees of living flesh, for what we call the circle of those of living flesh are as withered trees.
>
> Withered trees are the root of mindfulness. When we ourselves are groping about trying to hit the mark, this is mindfulness. There is the mindfulness when we have a body, as well as the mindfulness when our mind is free of attachments. There is the mindfulness of an involved mind, and there is the mindfulness when we go beyond body. The root of life of all humans on this great earth is the root of mindfulness, and the root of life of all the Buddhas in the ten quarters is the root of mindfulness. There are many people in one moment of mindfulness and there are many moments of mindfulness within one person... there is inexhaustible merit in being able to observe and thoroughly investigate this topic of mindfulness.[4]

When Dogen says, "There are many people in one moment of mindfulness," he points to what I am calling the "one-body, whole-life" manifestation of Zen. As the Buddha originally spoke of mindfulness, it was an individual practice. One developed moment-by-moment awareness of one's own body and mind. This awareness led to *vipassana*, or insight in the nature of reality, stepping onto the path of liberation—this is the root of most modern mindfulness practice. Dogen, however, is saying we wake up together, not individually.

In contemporary language, Zen Master Thich Nhat Hanh's classic *The Miracle of Mindfulness* asks about and explains this whole-life practice:

You might well ask: Then how are we to practice mindfulness?

My answer is: keep your attention focused on the work, be alert and able to handle ably and intelligently any situation which may arise—this is mindfulness. There is no reason why mindfulness should be different from focusing all one's attention on one's work, to be alert and to be using one's best judgment...

Mindfulness is the miracle by which we master and restore ourselves.[5]

Thich Nhat Hanh wrote this in a letter to a brother monk as bitter war continued in Vietnam's cities and countryside. Mindfulness was not easy to come by, and there was no place to sit peacefully outside the range of bombs and rifles. Mindfulness practice had to happen in the midst of life as it was.

Zen, as a school of Mahayana Buddhism, raises the bodhisattva ideal. From the realization of the interdependent nature of all life, a bodhisattva vows to awaken with all beings, deferring his or her own enlightenment until all can reach the other shore. The Vimalakirti Sutra offers this vision of the bodhisattva's work:

During the short aeons of swords,
They meditate on love,
Introducing to nonviolence
Hundreds of millions of living beings.

In the middle of great battles
They remain impartial to both sides;
For bodhisattvas of great strength
Delight in reconciliation of conflict.

In order to help the living beings,
They voluntarily descend into
The hells which are attached
To all the inconceivable buddha-fields.[6]

Thich Nhat Hanh writes in a similar vein:

> Mindfulness must be engaged. Once there is seeing, there must be acting. Otherwise, what is the use of seeing? We must be aware of the real problems of the world. Then, with mindfulness, we will know what to do and what not to do to be of help...[7]

This engagement is fully ethical; it is the expression of Buddha's precepts. Because it expresses the reality of interdependence and the inevitability of change, one moment of mindfulness contains, reflects, and influences the mindfulness of countless beings. Mindfulness is not one person's alone—it has a social and ethical dimension.

This can appear quite different from how mindfulness is currently marketed in the West. The modern "mindfulness movement" derives from Burmese Buddhist monastics, including Ledi Sayadaw, Mahasi Sayadaw, and others, who created a streamlined "vipassana" meditation in the late nineteenth century that appealed to monks and Burmese laypeople. This approach, transmitted to the US by a first generation of Western teachers, forms the basis for Jon Kabat-Zinn's system of Mindfulness-Based Stress Reduction (MBSR), developed at the University of Massachusetts over thirty years ago. Kabat-Zinn's approach rests on his own extensive Buddhist practice, but as its name implies it was secularized and carefully shaped for use in clinical settings as a means of stress management. We can interpret "stress" as another way to translate the Pali word *dukkha*.

Over the last ten or fifteen years, the teaching of mindfulness has proliferated. It has moved beyond the medical environment to schools, corporations, factories, prisons, and the military. In magazines and on bulletin boards, one can find instruction in mindful eating, psychology, childrearing, performance, sports, and much more.

Unlike Zen and many of the traditional approaches to Buddhism, where the development of teachers and the cultivation of wisdom can call for years of practice, there are few clear paths to authorization as a mindfulness teacher. Kabat-Zinn's MBSR program at the University of Massachusetts is an exception; it offers good training and certification. UCLA's Mindful Awareness Research Center also offers certification for trainers and teachers. These programs include intensive meditation, and consideration of ethical, psychological, and medical concerns for all practitioners. But too often an aspiring teacher takes a few classes, goes to some meditation sessions, and then hangs out a shingle as a mindfulness instructor, taking elements from here and there to craft a commercial program. As others have written in these pages, such approaches can easily become self-improvement projects, a commodity in the spirit of our new American religion, consumerism.

MBSR researchers Elizabeth Stanley and Amishi Jha, who have been working with the US Army, write:

> Mindfulness has been described as a process of "bringing one's attention to the present experience on a moment-by-moment basis" and as "paying attention in a particular way: on purpose, in the present moment and nonjudgmentally."[8]

But right mindfulness is not a context-less, bare awareness. There is a difference between acting "nonjudgmentally" and not using one's judgment. Mindfulness must contain the live fire of moral activity and wisdom.

When Jon Kabat-Zinn began to work on what would become MBSR, his previous training naturally led him along that threefold path. It is no surprise that in a recent interview Kabat-Zinn asserts:

> When we use the word mindfulness in MBSR, we mean right mindfulness. I use mindfulness as a kind of umbrella term. Woven into mindfulness is an orientation towards nonharming and seeing deeply into the nature of things, which in some way implies, or at least invites one, to see the interconnectedness between the seer and the seen, the object and the subject. It is a nondual perspective from the very beginning, resting on an ethical foundation.[9]

But this is where the critical question lies. Does a secular and mainstreamed "mindfulness movement" necessarily include the Buddhist precepts or an ethical foundation?

There is a strong critique of a deracinated and commodified approach to mindfulness in the West, clearly articulated by university professor Ron Purser and Zen teacher David Loy in their essay "Beyond McMindfulness":

> While a stripped-down, secularized technique—what some critics are now calling "McMindfulness"—may make it more palatable to the corporate world, decontextualizing mindfulness from its original liberative and transformative purpose, as well as its foundation in social ethics, amounts to a Faustian bargain. Rather than applying mindfulness as a means to awaken individuals and organizations from the unwholesome roots of greed, ill will and delusion, it is usually being refashioned into a banal, therapeutic, self-help technique that can actually reinforce those roots.

Later in this same essay, the authors quote Bhikkhu Bodhi:

> Absent a sharp social critique, Buddhist practices could easily be used to justify and stabilize the status quo, becoming a reinforcement of consumer capitalism.[10]

Mindfulness programs often not only are absent a sharp social critique but also are absent the training on the precepts. In recent years Google, General Mills, Procter & Gamble, Monsanto, and other corporate giants have hired mindfulness trainers to de-stress their employees. The development of mindfulness programs in corporate and military settings raises compelling ethical questions, including the problem of commodification. Corporate environments can be pressure cookers. The ability to practice meditation and mindfulness, even for the space of a few breaths, can immediately alter one's inner environment, which is part of the larger whole. In itself this is beneficial. But lacking a view of the precepts the question is not asked: What is the purpose of this corporation; what are we making?

In the Pali canon's Vanijja Sutta, the Buddha says:

> Monks, a lay follower should not engage in five types of business. Which five? Business in weapons, business in human beings, business in meat, business in intoxicants, and business in poison.[11]

By extension one might well consider the intoxicants of mass media, of expensive consumer goods marketed to children and adolescents, delusions purveyed by an education system that turns out cogs for the wheels of industry. Poisons? Tobacco, alcohol, and prescription drugs are advertised on prime time television.

The list goes on. Ordinary working people are employed in these industries. These are not fundamentally immoral people. But when they are taught meditative techniques like mindfulness, is there any attention given to the object of their labors? Are they asked to consider the actual things their corporation makes and sells—and whether it has a positive or negative social value?

Even for those who are working in education and healthcare—fields required for a harmonious society—is mindfulness taught in a way that reflects on dysfunctional organizational structures within which well-meaning employees are worn down to cynicism and powerlessness over the course of a career? In a world where "efficiency" rules, is mindfulness taught in a way that helps teachers and providers guard against tendencies to treat students and patients without sufficient regard for their true and human needs? If such matters are not surfaced, then "right" mindfulness is not being taught.

Different branches of the US military have been developing their own mindfulness programs, loosely based on approaches derived from MBSR. The US Army has its Comprehensive Soldier Fitness and Mindfulness-Based Mind Fitness Training (MMFT) programs. They have issued grants for $125 million to teach mindfulness, positive psychology, and resilience to more than a million troops.

According to researchers Stanley and Jha, the Army's MMFT program

is tailored for the military pre-deployment training cycle, with real-world examples from the counterinsurgency environment that show how mind fitness skills can enhance performance and mission accomplishment.[12]

Granted, there is a real concern and attention to harm-reduction here; mindfulness is being used as a tool in situations where stress and reactivity can lead to the death of innocents. Mindfulness can also be beneficial to veterans at home and their families, who can suffer the effects of violence and moral distress, what we have come to label posttraumatic stress disorder.

Still there is something chilling in Stanley and Jha's article, which is housed on the US Army's homepage. They present mindfulness as a technique of neuroplasticity so that "mind fitness training may provide 'mental armor' to protect troops as they prepare for deployment and experience the stressors of deployment itself."

> This concept is something athletes, musicians, and martial artists have known for a long time: with physical exercise and repetition of certain body movements, the body becomes stronger, more efficient, and better able to perform those movements with ease. A similar process can occur with the brain: with the engagement and repetition of certain mental processes, the brain becomes more efficient at those processes... In other words, experience and training can lead to functional and structural reorganization of the brain.[13]

I read this as an argument for building better war-fighters. And I can't help thinking that once the "functional and structural reorganization of the brain" has been accomplished, it cannot be easily undone.

Having raised the flag of Zen as one-body, whole-life practice I must step back and note that Zen also provides an example of what can happen when a practice is appropriated for narrow societal (and especially military) ends. Zen has its own dark history, growing out of Japan's feudal past and the samurai warrior's code. Leading Zen teachers and schools—along with other schools of Japanese Buddhism—bear responsibility for terrible atrocities in Japan's military occupations and wars with Russia, China, Manchuria, and Korea before and during World War II. The formulation of an "Imperial Way Zen" melded the Buddhist principles of selflessness, discipline, and mindfulness with the aggressive goals of an expansionist, militarist state, concocting a witch's brew of violent nationalism.[14]

Without delving too far into the controversies surrounding particular teachers, it is clear that Zen and Japanese militarism were at ease with each other. In 1905, at the time of the Russo-Japanese war, D. T. Suzuki's teacher Soen Shaku—who served as a combat chaplain to Japanese troops in Manchuria—wrote:

> The hand that is raised to strike and the eye that is fixed to take aim, do not belong to the individual, but are instruments utilized by a principle higher than transient existence.[15]

This is the mystification of a soldier's world, the culmination of mindfulness as technique, far from the moral integrity of Buddha's path. When examined as a distinct system or social structure, an army, a prison, and a corporation each has its own internal ethical principles. Many of these principles are admirable and potentially protective of individuals in lower and higher positions within that organization, but these systems too often stop at the front door. Because they look inwardly but not outwardly at the way that system, structure, or organization relates to the larger world, they fail to accomplish the Buddha's way.

To move from abstract to particular, here are some specific questions worth raising before applying mindfulness to any and all settings:

- If one is practicing mindfulness in a corporation, what are you making and selling, how are you treating your workers in a distant land, and at what cost are you extracting resources from the earth?
- If one is working in a prison, on either side of the bars, do you see the common humanity of prisoners, guards, and administrators?
- If one is bringing mindfulness programs to active-duty soldiers, what if they are taking part in wars that might be viewed as illegal and unwinnable, and what does it mean to take orders and direction from a political structure that is not accountable for the widespread violence of its own policies?
- And finally: Before we minister to corporations, prisons, and the military, perhaps we should consider that the members of our government and the policy makers on corporate boards and in the so-called justice system are the ones who most need instruction in right mindfulness.

CONCLUSION

The mainstreaming of mindfulness is a remarkable phenomenon. It may be around for the long run. For what it's worth, capitalism is also a remarkable and voracious force. Many of the radical cultural shifts of the late twentieth century that seemed to portend social revolution are now comfortably folded into the consumer marketplace. Along with the co-optations of "greenwashing" and the pronouncements that our society is supposedly "post-racial" and "post-feminist," mindfulness runs the risk of being the next big thing to be folded into the consumer marketplace. Alas.

In a recent Facebook posting, the contemporary writer and teacher Stephen Batchelor suggests:

> This moment of broad interest and sympathy for a core Buddhist practice presents the Buddhist community with an extraordinary window of opportunity. The challenge now is to do for Buddhist ethics and philosophy what Kabat-Zinn and others have done for Buddhist meditation. But this will require, I believe, the courage to radically rethink what the Dharma is about.[16]

Batchelor is certainly right that courage is required to meet our hazardous future. But I wonder if he's right that we need "to radically rethink what the Dharma is about." It is about liberation and always has been. From the Buddha's time it offered a path for men and women, monks, and nuns, people of all castes. Its view is wide and deep, looking beyond the barriers of greed, hatred, and delusion.

As I wrote earlier, while we translate *sammasati* as "right mindfulness," one can also translate it as "right remembering" or "right recollecting": remembering where we are this moment, remembering what we value in ourselves and others, remembering how to live. We will re-collect our lives as one body again and again for the sake of all beings. We must.

6. THE BUFFET
ADVENTURES IN THE NEW AGE

Sallie Jiko Tisdale

Several years ago, I was asked to teach a workshop in memoir at the Omega Institute for Holistic Studies, as part of their annual Arts Week. Somehow I had never heard of Omega, one of the biggest purveyors of New Age experience in the country, so they sent me a catalog. The classes and workshops were a hodgepodge collection, and many were registered trademarks. Over the years, along with conferences on women's leadership and workshops in sustainability, Omega has offered training in Egyptian healing rods, Quantum Resonance, past-life regression, voodoo, Chakra balancing, juice fasts, harmonic resonance, VortexHealing®, Toltec wisdom, Warrior Goddess Training, the divine Merlin lineage, weight loss, Tantric sexuality, Tree Whispering®, Tennis Inside the Zone, herbal skin care, Trance Mediumship, and Boot Camp for Goddesses®.

Not surprising, then, that Omega offers a lot of mindfulness workshops: the Mindfulness & Education Conference, the Science of Mindfulness, Mindful Running for Beginners, Mindfulness & Writing, Bringing Mindfulness to Work, Mindfulness Exercises for Kids, Mindfulness Is Like Coffee, Mindfulness-Based Relapse Prevention (MBRP), Mindfulness-Based Eating Awareness Training (MB-EAT), Mindfulness-Based Cognitive Therapy

(MBCT), Mindfulness-Based Stress Reduction (MBSR), and of course, Mindfulness for Everyone. There's more, but I quit reading.

Well, I thought, at least it's Arts Week. I spoke with a staff person several times to work out the details. We agreed on a fee. I asked for a quiet room with a blackboard and tables. She offered me a room with pillows on the floor, but I wanted the tables. I asked for a maximum of twelve students; she wanted me to take twenty, and we settled on fifteen.

On a hot Sunday afternoon in July, I arrived at the Hudson Valley campus—two hundred bucolic acres of grass and trees with an old lodge, a gymnasium, and rows of white-washed cabins. I was shown to a spare, pleasant room, looking down toward the gardens.

That night, everyone came to the gymnasium for orientation. In the sick, humid heat, more than three hundred people milled around in quiet excitement. The teachers were introduced. Besides memoir writing, Arts Week included workshops in tango, improvisational comedy, songwriting, African drumming, belly-dancing, gospel singing, and inexplicably, trapeze. I stood when it was my turn and looked over a sea of strangers, and every one of them was smiling.

Several streams of influence have defined my adult years: Zen Buddhism, writing, rearing children, the community development movement. I began to identify with the counterculture in adolescence, at the tail end of the 1960s. When I was seventeen, I moved to Eugene, Oregon, where a lot of smart, creative longhairs had built an interlocking web of nonprofits and co-ops. I volunteered at the food co-op and the women's health clinic and worked for a juvenile justice project. I was years younger than everyone else in the room, and I learned through osmosis—especially through countless hours in meetings, where people ten and twenty years my senior talked, argued, and came to terms with each other and with the way the world worked and the ways in which it was possible to change it.

I realized that I wanted to be a writer, and to do that, I needed a steady job. I started nursing school and I also started a family, and in the midst of those stressful years, I uncovered a powerful religious impulse that had been briefly buried in political work. I began to practice Zen Buddhism, which quickly became the central explanation of my life.

All the realms in which I worked—nursing and parenting included—require discipline, patience, and delayed gratification. Activism involves near-constant collisions with the assumptions of mainstream culture, and frequent compromise. I studied Zen with serious teachers who had decades of monastic training behind them—a precise, disciplined, and surprisingly hardheaded practice rooted in the ordinary. I see now the similarities in my varied passions: a focus on the tasks of daily life, the work required to sustain community, the private struggle and the long view. While to an outsider any of these worlds can look exotic, there is something prairie-plain about them all.

The creeping fascination with what is called New Age philosophy had nothing to do with such labors. I didn't pay any attention to the movement for years, until I began to notice the way words like *karma* and *Zen* were sliding into conversations, without seeming to mean what I thought they meant. *Mindfulness* became a slang word for everything from silence to mild group therapy.

I'm allergic to phrases like "paranormal scanning" and "discovering your soul mission" and to the idea that you can practice telepathy on your pets. I distrust any lineup of "tribal wisdom keepers" and "global evolutionary leaders" trained in the "Sacred Transmissions" of various lands who make grand promises about transformation over the course of a weekend. I'm averse to the chopped-up mystery meat of ideas that insists so much on absolute ends and perfect means, on universal light and universal love and universal energy and surprisingly easy ways to get them.

In fact I believe in things like complete awakening and universal energy. But I also believe in methods that may be easy to learn but are tough to master, and I believe in decades of practice at them. (Mindfulness is a perfect example of such a method.) I believe that human lives are bound to include struggle and suffering and that anyone who smiles all the time is hiding something.

Writing workshops are difficult and unnatural. They require long hours wrestling with one's own stilted words in solitude, more long hours in a chair listening to someone else's often stilted effort, and they do this at an unnaturally fast pace. I have always approached my own workshops with ambivalence and nerves. I don't really believe you can teach people to write—but still, I've witnessed a lot of small miracles in writing workshops over the years. A few of my students have become writers after all, and many of the others have taken the lessons of writing—the humility, courage, and willingness of the writer—into the rest of their lives.

Part of my vague disquiet at trying to teach writing at a place like Omega was how often New Age thinking makes reference to "creativity" and uses the artistic impulse as a tool for so-called transformation. The sweaty problem of the narrative or the fine charcoal line doesn't, in my experience, have much to do with a mission like Omega's—to "explore the extraordinary potential that exists in all of us as individuals and together as a human family" and "the holistic worldview that the well-being of each of us is deeply connected to the well-being of all living things." As nice as that sounds.

When I arrived at my first workshop session on Monday morning, I found twenty-nine students and a technician setting up a video camera and recording equipment. I insisted that the camera and recorders had to go, setting off a flurry of distress in the young staff. During the noon break, I went to the office to explain that my written contract stipulated fifteen students. The first young woman told me brightly, as though I were a bit slow, "But you're paid per student!" The second woman met me with a serene smile that tightened in a wave of disapproval as I spoke—there and gone almost before I could see it, as though I'd farted in church.

I got rid of the video, but I was stuck with twenty-nine students.

At Omega, I was surprised to discover that noise was a constant feature—layered voices carried through the hazy air day and night, along with radios, basketballs bouncing off the outdoor court, flutes and violins playing scales by the pond, children hollering. The drums pounded, near and far, at all hours—sudden rapping staccatos, rhythmic bass beats, complex melodies, and sometimes a whole chorus rattling through the trees. The bookstore was always busy: it sold CDs, candles, clothing, incense, videotapes, and books on all manner of things. The students could take morning and evening tai chi and yoga, or a trapeze lesson, or take labyrinth walks. They could get a massage at the Wellness Center, followed by a session of astrology.

The word holistic was coined by the forgotten South African military leader Jan Christian Smuts in 1926 in his book *Holism and Evolution*. (The bookstore had *Zen Guitar* and *The Pocket Guide to the Chakras* but nothing by J. C. Smuts.) He believed that the components of reality are fundamentally whole in themselves, not merely parts of something else. Smuts tackled Darwin, psychoanalysis, cellular biology, sociology, and the mechanics of space and time in his book. Because what seems to be a "part" is really a "whole," Smuts wrote, all things are fluid and adaptable, constantly changing in their qualities. Smuts felt that seeing the mind holistically required a belief in a consciousness beyond the brain, since chemicals and neurons are also whole things. Mostly Smuts didn't make a lot of sense, though his intentions seem to have been good, and he set a standard for grandiosity that is carried forward by his philosophical descendants today. He believed he'd found the solution to the long war between religion and science. His ideas came down to a theory of everything, and in the theory of everything, anything goes.

Poor old Smuts thought that every part was a whole. But the New Age is all about parts—taking bits of this and that as we please. To really treat anything or any person holistically requires a lot of attention and time— it means honoring each thing *as it is*, completely, rather than taking it apart. The mix of people I found at Omega seemed diverse on first glance: a few African women in colorful turbans and scruffy young fellows in balloon pants and crocheted berets. Grey-haired men in neatly pressed Hawaiian shirts and grey-haired women in bright batik blouses. Young maidens with silver balls winking in their nostrils, their shoulders slipping out of baby-doll dresses. The tango students wore slacks, wide skirts, patent-leather shoes. The belly dancers wrapped colorful scarves over their shoulders and came to meals self-consciously barefoot, tinkling their new ankle bells. A group of lithe people with small, smug smiles and skin-tight spandex turned out to be the trapeze instructors. I saw caps, rosaries, beads, shirts, and jewelry from the Caribbean, Tibet, Kenya, Guatemala, China, Ecuador. Instead of seeing each thing in the world as a whole, we've come to see each thing in the world as a piece for the taking. Thus, religious instruction is a smattering of what is so often called the "world's wisdom traditions," over a long weekend, with the more disturbing parts

surgically removed. Kabbalah without Orthodoxy. Voodoo without sacrifice. Zen without morality. We are hungry to believe, sometimes frantic
to believe—to believe in something, anything, to be guided, taught what
is missing. That means the willingness to try anything except sticking to
one path for life, anything but the boredom and struggle of commitment
to a single way.

On second glance, people at Omega were far more similar than different. Almost all the young people were staff. Almost everyone else was, like
me, white, middle aged, and well fed. The Africans were part of the gospel
group or the drumming instructor's entourage.

I felt awkward, out of step, a little cranky and lonesome. (My penchant
for cheap jokes was definitely out of place.) Each request I made—for use
of a copy machine, for instance—fell into the staff's new image of me. I
was "her, again." I began to see that expressing a need was suspect. Asking for something implies that the world is imperfect; my smallest request
seemed out of place in paradise. My biggest mistake seemed to be that I'd
made plans.

I couldn't remember my twenty-nine students' names. I kept redoing the
syllabus, and I spent most of the hours outside class trying to read so many
stories. I grew tired of the minutely labeled, warning-ridden food in the
dining hall. I was tired of the small smiles, the careful speech, the pervasive
lack of wit. I missed silence. I discovered a lovely meditation hall up the
hill—where there was, of course, a labyrinth—and started walking up each
morning to do zazen. But each time I went, there were already people there,
talking—talking about light, talking about energy, talking about God. Or
just talking. Sometimes on cell phones.

The real agenda of the New Age is not self-fulfillment but self-comfort.
If it doesn't feel good—well, $1,500 a week should buy some ease. The
world is a buffet, and its adherents fill their plates according to appetite. In
this New Age, we are expected to embrace diversity but blur our distinctions—forget our differences but celebrate the unknown. At a buffet, one
wants to taste everything—because one is *supposed* to taste everything, not
miss anything. When mindfulness practice, an ancient discipline rooted in
demanding religious traditions, is appropriated by the New Age, it becomes
an exercise in self-satisfaction rather than self-awareness.

I hitched a ride from the dry campus into town with one of my students and came back with a couple of bottles of wine.

Omega was founded in 1977 by Elizabeth Lesser and Stephan Rechtschaffen, inspired by Sufi meditation teacher Pir Vilayat Inayat Khan, but for a long time, Lesser has been its public face. Lesser has called her religious practice a kind of "serial monogamy"—she is a long-time student of Sufism, but she says she has also practiced Tibetan Buddhism, Zen Buddhism, Christian mysticism, "bodywork," mythology, and Jungian analysis in her pursuit of truth. She calls this a "self-regulated kind of spirituality"—to stick to one religion over a lifetime is, she has said, immature; it shows an inability to keep growing. Lesser sings in a church choir, but she doesn't like "rule-based theologies" that limit behavior, because so many people have told her of their "reluctance to engage with organized religions if it meant they had to make an exclusive commitment." She doesn't believe in "blame or shame or guilt and the strange proscriptions that humans devise to prevent or punish the evil that dwells within each of our hearts."[1]

Omega is more mainstream than it used to be, with lots of yoga workshops and kids' art classes, conferences on leadership, programs specifically for veterans, and the many versions of copyrighted mindfulness practice. Lesser herself seems to have matured into a slightly more questioning philosophy. She likes lists, and one of them is "Spiritual Materialism's Top-Ten List," which includes believing in "Instant Transformation," a "Desire for Magic," "Romanticizing Indigenous Cultures," and "Ripping Off the Traditions." Yet she's gotten rich and powerful on exactly these things. She has built an international career on the human longing to find a ground in which to plant our lives, and the human impatience with how long that takes.

The very difficulty of staying the course is a crucial part of a spiritual practice—and its own reward, no matter the path. Like staying with a relationship through times of boredom and fear, staying with a religion through time is the only way to confront certain truths about one's self and what we call the divine. In the end, my main objection to the patchwork offerings of the New Age—including the use of mindfulness as a means to personal enrichment—is that I just don't believe it works. Nothing much is learned by sampling.

If the world's wisdom traditions have anything to teach, if there is a truth that seems to cross methodology, it is this: stick to one thing. Say *yes* to something in particular—which means you must mostly say *no* to everything else. Every wisdom tradition I know promises the opposite of an easy road: that discomfort and fulfillment lie side by side, entwined with scary and sometimes lonely inner work. Like art, religion is as much as anything else about the long haul.

This comes together in one peculiar tension point: if you want a master's wisdom but you don't want to put in the lifetime of work needed to develop it, you can hire the master. Wisdom traditions don't spring up overnight—not real ones, at least. New Age consumers appropriate the labor of many other people who've done the hard work: their apprenticeship, their lives of study—*their* tedium, *their* commitment. What is appropriated most of all is the same thing colonialists have always taken: other people's time, the hard, long years of those who weren't in such a big hurry.

All religion, by its nature, deals in powerful, dark material at times. Whether it's possible to gain anything from a weekend workshop is one question—whether it is even good to teach certain practices seems not to be considered. Thus we can take the Shamanic Journey, Evolutionary Shamanism, Advanced Applied Shamanism, or the Great Shamanic Initiation—"Together we experience energetic transmissions of an ancient Inca lineage of earth-keepers during two fire ceremonies. These transmissions help us grow a body that heals and ages differently, and allow us to dream a new world into being. The Andean shamans… also provide an updated and live reading of their prophecies beyond 2015."[2]—without worrying about what shamanism, divorced from culture and language and history, becomes. Practices of power learned out of context are a little like dynamite, if they work at all. Is Incan shamanism the best spiritual path for the elementary school teacher from Brooklyn and the retired dentist in Hoboken? I don't even hear the question being asked.

In spite of its sheer size, in spite of students coming and going at will, the noise and ceaseless distractions, a bit of magic emerged in the workshop. Pellucid moments: a hushed reading when everyone suddenly sat up and paid attention at once, the sudden dawn across a clenched face. The pleasure in simply saying what is true. The satisfaction unlike any other I've known when the obstacles dissolve like sand in a wave, when *language* becomes a natural force pouring out of your hands.

One day a staff person showed up at the start of the class.

"Remember, everyone performs on Friday night," she announced. No one had mentioned this before. I protested that we weren't engaged in a performing art. My students were working on rough drafts of memoirs: long, loose pages, much of it raw and very personal.

"It's a tradition," the young woman told me, as though traditions were common around there. At the end of the week, the belly dancers would dance, the comedians would perform a skit, the songwriters would sing their songs. I briefly considered a little guerilla theatre: all of us lounging around the stage writing silently in our notebooks for ten minutes and then taking a bow. But instead I changed my plans again, and we started polishing short sections to read aloud.

The performance went about as well as I expected—a twilight trapeze demonstration for a clapping crowd on the lawn; a shy, bouncy belly dance; a slick tango or two; several brand-new songs. And several of my brave students stood up with shaking hands and read in timid voices about accidents and confusion and loss and were politely applauded by the bewildered audience.

The next evening, the last of the week, is a concert by Sister Alice Williams, the gospel teacher.

Hundreds of people crowd the hall and fill every chair and aisle. Sister Alice is a big, self-confident woman who wears a rainbow-colored caftan in layers that drift and float in the steamy summer night. Her black hair is carefully coiffed, solid and glossy, and she wears thick glasses that catch the small stage lights and flash like mirrors.

Of all things here, gospel! Soaring hope made out of the human burden, a music about loving and serving the God of the Bible and no other gods. Gospel is about being good and obeying the rules, and its purpose is to evangelize. Sister Alice and her unreprobate Christian music celebrates divine commandments, and she is doing it in a place that rejects the very idea of commandments. Gospel is *church*.

She starts by singing songs familiar to many of us from summer camps that offered a lot of Peter, Paul, and Mary. Between songs, she preaches—she cajoles and hectors and points her finger.

"Don't be a fool!" she shouts, "Come now, children, don't be fools!"

The crowd embraces Sister Alice.

She is leading us up an arc of growing noise and energy—loud and then soft and then tugging us in. Fast, happy songs give way to slow, contemplative call-and-response, an increasingly fast alteration like the roar of a coming train. The people around me begin to hum, then sing along, then tentatively wave and sway, still uncertain of what's correct, what's done—what might offend. Does something real remain when we take a small piece? If everything is made of wholes, perhaps it does. I suppose God would know what Sister Alice and her family think of this sea of prosperous pale skin. Do they see an ocean of sinners and potential converts, or a week's good wages? Does anyone really want to know?

And what the hell—in the back, where people are dancing, I start to let go. We can all use a cure for self-satisfaction, myself most certainly included. There is, I'm sure, a lot of sincerity here—charlatans and snake oil, but sincere seekers too. And at least some of this is truth—offered in digestible bites, trademarked and sold for profit, but true nonetheless.

And I have been a seeker, too; I am a seeker still. Even if I've found my trail, I don't know where it ends. The Wiccans are clapping and the shamans are swaying and a lot of Jews are calling "Hallelujah!" In front of me a tender young thing in a long skirt with a silky bare midriff as unmarred as a blue sky undulates dreamily with her eyes closed, while all around her people are tapping their feet and shyly saying "Amen!" and Sister Alice's mother is in the aisles pulling people out of their chairs and pretty soon everyone is having a really good time.

Cheerfully ignoring everything that has come before and everything that must follow, Sister Alice sings and all the aerial flyers and labyrinth walkers and even my own grumpy self are calling on *Jeeesus's name*; we're putting *God!* in our hearts and our hands in the hand of *the maaan from Gaalllillleee*. For a little while. For now.

"Darling," calls Sister Alice, "You can do it!"

Tomorrow we can try something new.

PART II

CREATIVE ENGAGEMENT

Zen Experiences with Mindfulness Practice

7. TWO PRACTICES, ONE PATH

Gil Fronsdal and Max Erdstein

Monks, this is the direct path for the purification of beings, for the surmounting of sorrow and lamentation, for the disappearance of suffering and discontent, for acquiring the true method, for the realization of Nibbana, namely, the four foundations of mindfulness.

—Satipatthana Sutta[1]

One day a man of the people said to Zen Master Ikkyu: "Master, will you please write for me some maxims of the highest wisdom?" Ikkyu immediately took his brush and wrote the word "Attention." "Is that all?" asked the man. "Will you not add something more?" Ikkyu then wrote twice running: "Attention. Attention." "Well," remarked the man rather irritably, "I really don't see much depth or subtlety in what you have just written." Then Ikkyu wrote the same word three times running: "Attention. Attention. Attention." Half angered, the man demanded: "What does that word 'Attention' mean anyway?" And Ikkyu answered gently: "Attention means attention."

—Phillip Kapleau, *The Three Pillars of Zen*[2]

INTRODUCTION

By Max Erdstein

How does the quality of "attention," as cultivated in Zen training, relate to the faculty of "mindfulness," which was extolled by the Buddha as the direct path to awakening?

The three pieces that follow aim to move us closer to the answer to this question by looking at the development of this quality of mind, sati, usually translated as "mindfulness," from three perspectives. "Awareness or Clear Comprehension" is a close textual reading of how "mindfulness" is understood within the teachings of the Buddha in the Pali suttas; "When Mindfulness Is Too Much" shares a personal journey into the depths of meditation from the vantage point of a meditator who practiced within both the Zen and Theravada traditions; and "The Zen of Vipassana" is a conversation between two teachers in the Insight Meditation tradition who are deeply influenced by Zen practice.

Vipassana is a Pali word that means "clear seeing," which refers to the insight that results from its practice: clearly seeing the nature of conditioned phenomena. The basis for practicing clear seeing is the knowing faculty of mind, sati, usually translated as "mindfulness"; mindfulness meditation matures into vipassana.

Vipassana meditation instructions come directly from the Satipatthana Sutta, which presents a systematic way one can establish mindfulness for the purpose of insight, letting go, and awakening. Although the Satipatthana Sutta is the foundational Theravadin text for the Western Insight Meditation movement, I was first taught it in-depth during a three-month practice period at Tassajara, a Zen monastery. From this study, I discovered that the Buddha's practice of "right mindfulness" refers to a knowing, observing, and essentially wholesome quality of mind, which is necessarily free from the filters of greed, hate, and delusion. Suzuki Roshi said as much when he declared, "All precepts are included in zazen."

In the years since, I have been happily engaged in the exploration of how this quality of mind is established, developed, and matured in both the Zen and Vipassana models of practice. Zen training imprints a certain way of being present: wholeheartedly, with sensitivity, and genuine unconditional acceptance. I recall the careful and continuous attention to posture, the nondiscriminatory mind of zazen, and the graceful choreography of zendo rituals. Vipassana practice demands a precise, microscopic focus on the bare elements of moment-to-moment experience, deconstructing the process of mind and body.

Outwardly different, these two may offer complementary routes to the Buddhist goal of freedom from suffering. When I wondered how I might integrate these two approaches, I asked Gil Fronsdal, my teacher, "Where do Zen and Vipassana come together?" He responded, "Hopefully in you, in your body."

Gil answers this question with some authority, being both a transmitted Zen teacher, in the lineage of Sojun Mel Weitsman and Suzuki Roshi, as well as a senior Vipassana teacher, who practiced in Burma under Sayadaw U Pandita and was trained to teach by Jack Kornfield. Gil has also studied the primary texts deeply; he has a doctorate in Buddhist studies from Stanford.

This period of Dharma practice in the West is a time of abundance. We have various Buddhist traditions operating side by side, as siblings and peaceful neighbors. Hopefully Zen and Vipassana will continue offering what makes each unique and valuable, while also learning from each other, when appropriate. This can happen precisely because Zen and Vipassana don't exist in the abstract; each zendo and Vipassana community is a local experiment, inviting us to step beyond the stuffy world of our preferences and into the cool breeze of reality, life as it truly is.

AWARENESS OR CLEAR COMPREHENSION: SATI IN THE BUDDHA'S TEACHINGS
by Gil Fronsdal

The image that most universally represents Buddhism is that of the Buddha meditating. Without the Buddha's awakening, there would be no Buddhism, and without meditation, there would be no awakening. Even as an awakened being, the Buddha is often depicted in the scriptures as spending a good portion of his days in meditation, i.e., doing the "day's abiding."[3]

One of the words most closely connected to the Buddha's meditation is *sati*, which is usually translated as "mindfulness." But it may not be the best choice; the modern Western meanings of "mindfulness" may not be a good match for how sati is used in the ancient Buddhist texts. In the following discussion, I will begin by avoiding using "mindfulness" and instead relying on the Pali word *sati* so we can better look at its meaning in a fresh way.

THE MENTAL FACULTY OF SATI

In the early Pali discourses the concept of sati is used in two broad, overlapping ways: the mental faculty of sati, and the practice of sati. The distinct role in the course of meditation of these two aspects of sati is often obscured because it is easy to conflate them.

As a mental faculty sati is one of the five mental faculties, or *indriyas*, that is, faith, energy, sati, concentration, and wisdom.

As is true with many terms, the Buddhist discourses do not provide a detailed definition or explanation for the faculty of sati. Therefore to understand what this faculty is we have to rely on how the word is used in the ancient texts.

One way of understanding what sati might be is through the relationship one can have with it. In the Buddha's teachings this is described as follows:

- One *possesses* sati[4]
- One *is endowed with* sati[5]
- One *has purity of* sati[6]
- One *is established in* sati[7]
- One *abides in* sati[8]

In the first three of these statements sati is something one has. In the last two it is a state within which one is. Nowhere does the Buddha specifically instruct others to actively apply or do sati; sati is a noun not a verb. There is one passage where the Buddha says he "arouses sati" in his monastic disciples,[9] but while this may mean he instructs them to do sati, it could also mean that he evokes a state of sati in them.

Overall the discourses give the impression that sati is an important faculty that a person possesses but is not a mental activity a person intentionally engages in. In this sense the faculty of sati may be similar to the faculty of faith: while one can have faith and one can develop faith, faith is not something one does. The words *sati* and *saddha* (faith) are both nouns referring to faculties one possesses or can be established in, not something that is actively practiced.

So when the Buddha instructs monastics to make an effort to develop sati or to evaluate whether it is developed in them,[10] he is not telling them to engage in the activity of mindfulness; rather he is telling them to engage in activities that strengthen the faculty of sati. This is why the Buddha explains the development of sati through activities other than sati itself. In other words, sati is a result of other practices.

Given that the most common usage of the word *sati* is in the descriptions of the third and fourth *jhana*, advanced states of meditative absorption, to understand what sati might be we also need to understand it in this context. In neither of these two meditative states is a person actively doing or applying mindfulness. Instead, sati is simply present.

Because of this, a better translation for sati than "mindfulness" might be "awareness"—a word I associate with a state of receptive attentiveness not requiring self-conscious effort. In this sense, "awareness" generally fits the various ways sati is used in the suttas better than does "mindfulness." This also means that traditionally sati had a different meaning than how mindfulness is usually taught today, when it is used more as an active practice of directed attention; for example, when one chooses to be mindful of something.

The overall impression from the suttas is that the faculty of sati as a capacity for being aware is an important mental state that is evoked or developed through particular practices. Because they set up or establish awareness, these practices can be called "the practice of sati," "awareness practices," or "practices for establishing awareness."

THE PRACTICE OF SATI

If we look at the teachings of the Buddha, we see that the *practice* of sati involves more than the particular *faculty* of sati; it includes a combination of practices and faculties.

The distinction between the faculty of sati and practice of sati can be illustrated with an analogy. Someone who has the ability to walk may walk in many different ways. One way might be to train for a long hike, in which case the person's practice of walking develops his or her faculty of walking: one's ability to walk improves. The person's walking practice may vary in frequency and intensity; it may involve walking fast and far enough to build stamina and strength. It may involve choosing to alternate between walking in hills and walking on flat land. In a similar way we have the ability to be aware. Particular forms of practice that involve more than simply being aware can strengthen this ability. This can include frequent and ardent attentional exercises, actively letting go of thoughts that obscure present moment awareness, and choosing helpful areas of life to focus attention.

The practice of Right Sati, the seventh factor in the Eightfold Path, is described accordingly:

What, friends, is right sati? Here a monk abides observing the body as body, with ardency, clear comprehension, and awareness, having put away covetousness and grief for the world. He abides observing feeling tones as feeling tones, with ardency, clear comprehension, and awareness, having put away covetousness and grief for the world. He abides observing mind states as mind states, with ardency, clear comprehension, and awareness, having put away covetousness and grief for the world. He abides observing mind objects as mind objects, with ardency, clear comprehension, and awareness, having put away covetousness and grief for the world.[11]

Here sati practice involves observing four particular areas of experience: the body, feeling tones, mind states, and mind objects. Second, it includes doing so with ardency, clear comprehension, and awareness. Third, it requires "having put away covetousness and grief for the world."

In this quote, which is my translation, the word "awareness" serves as the translation of *sati*. Most English translations of this passage render *sati* as "mindfulness." Regardless of how it is translated, the word is used to characterize *how* to practice observing. In other words, sati is not a practice; rather it is a manner of how to practice.

The Buddha's most important teachings on sati are found in a text popularly called the *Discourse on the Foundations of Mindfulness*.[12] This text contains no instructions to actively practice mindfulness or to direct mindfulness. In fact, given that sati is in the title of the text, the word *sati* is, surprisingly, mostly absent in the discourse. Instead of providing instructions in "doing" mindfulness, the text instructs us to do such intentional activities as observe, understand, relax, clearly comprehend, and review.

This gets more interesting when we consider the phrase commonly translated as "foundations of mindfulness": *satipatthana*. While *sati* can mean "awareness," it is not clear what *patthana* means. One of the primary choices is "establishing." *Satipatthana* thereby would be "establishing awareness," and the full title of the text could be the *Discourse on Establishing Awareness*. The instruction given in the text is how to establish a heightened attentiveness or wakefulness through a variety of different practices, all of which should be practiced with ardency, clear comprehension, and awareness.

If *sati* is best translated as "awareness," then *sampajanna*, the Pali word for "clear comprehension," is a better fit for the English word "mindfulness." This is because in contemporary mindfulness teaching "mindfulness" often involves clearly knowing what one is aware of. That is, when one is mindful, one clearly comprehends whatever is the focus of attention. In other words, in modern teachings, "mindfulness" often corresponds to the Buddhist concept of *sampajanna*, not *sati*.

When this clear comprehension / mindfulness (*sampajanna*) is combined with ardency, awareness (sati), and the observation of body, feeling tones, mind states, and mind objects, this set of practices can still be known as "mindfulness practice." However, the designation comes from my proposed translation of *sampajanna*, not that of *sati*.

Regardless of how we translate the ancient Buddhist words, the purpose of mindfulness practice is to establish a strong degree of awareness. This, in turn, can lead to a state that the *Discourse on the Establishing of Awareness* describes as "abiding independent, not clinging to anything in the world."[13] When awareness becomes strong and stable one can enter and abide in it in such a way that one can find freedom from what is known. The *Discourse on the Establishing of Awareness* ends by stating:

This is the direct path for the purification of beings, for overcoming sorrow and lamentation, for the disappearance of distress and grief, for the attainment of the practice, for the realization of *Nibbana*—namely, the four ways of establishing awareness.[14]

WHEN MINDFULNESS IS TOO MUCH[15]
by Gil Fronsdal

Surprisingly, the day came when I had to give up mindfulness. While this was temporary, it proved to be a necessary step in my path toward liberation. To show how this was the case, I will explain a bit of my history with Buddhist practice.

Before practicing mindfulness in Theravada Buddhism, I spent years practicing Zen. I remain very grateful for my early years of Zen training; it was a remarkable training in being present for life. First, I learned a lot about how I was not present. As I learned to be more attentive to my present-moment experience, I then learned a lot about how I reacted for and against this experience. Slowly I learned to be present without any observable reactivity. I understood this nonreactivity as a practice of unconditional acceptance in which experiences were allowed to exist in an open awareness.

In the course of this Zen training I had a range of meaningful experiences. I not only came to understand something of the interconnected aspect of our life and world, I had insights where this was seen in vivid and awe-inspiring clarity. Other times my experience could not be described in the usual subject-object perspective; refreshingly, I was not aware of any sense of self in the very intimate flow of experience.

I came to value the Zen approach that everything was practice—that everything that was happening was something to offer my full presence to.

But I noticed some of my fellow Zen practitioners' ideas about Zen practice were different from mine. In particular, some students believed that there was one thing we were not supposed to be present for, either because it did not exist or because it was second-best or somehow wrong to experience. The unacceptable experience or transformation was any that could be labeled "enlightenment." Some Zen friends had the attitude that the only thing to do with a so-called enlightenment experience was to let it go and preferably forget all about it as we moved into the next moment with full awareness. Others believed there was no such thing as enlightenment as a clear and dramatic transformative experience. Or if there was enlightenment, it was not the radical, life-altering experience some people reported. Rather it was any moment in the course of ordinary life when there was no subject-object distinction or there was some meaningful level of acceptance and peace.

While I did not know what enlightenment might be, I was confused by ideas that seemed to belittle or dismiss it. I was even more confused knowing how important enlightenment was for the Buddha and for much of Buddhism.

After my Zen training, I engaged in intensive Vipassana training in Burma. The mindfulness practice I was taught there helped me to see that the acceptance I had experienced through Zen was not as thorough an acceptance as I had believed. Through careful and sustained mindfulness I saw an array of subtle—almost underground—thoughts and intentions that were not accepting. For example, I was sometimes able to sit with open acceptance of my anger. However, when I looked carefully I saw that the anger itself was a symptom of some nonacceptance. Or I saw in the gaps of my thinking that there were underlying, hidden feelings of fear, striving, or self-referencing. My mind had to be very still to see the subtle operation of greed, hate, and delusion, as well as to sense the agitation and constriction they caused.

As my mind became more still and quiet, I became aware that it seemed to have a natural inclination to let go of the increasingly subtle agitation that remained. From the perspective of ordinary life, my mind was now very serene. Even so, similar to the way a very still lake highlights the slightest ripple, so deep meditation revealed the slightest movements of mind.

And similar to the way water will flow downhill if unimpeded, so I found an almost inherent momentum for the mind to move toward stillness, to let go of even the smallest agitation. As I allowed for this slide into greater stillness, I discovered that many of my cherished ideas and meditation experiences involved movements of the mind. Feelings of oneness, interconnectedness, compassion, bliss, and no-self all involved very subtle movements of mind that interfered with greater stillness.

I also learned that, at times, any effort to practice was more mental movement. I was fine with letting go of effort—I had come to value effortlessness in my Zen practice. But I was not at first prepared to let go of mindfulness. Mindfulness seemed like the core of the practice. But when I understood that mindfulness was itself an activity of the mind, I could feel a desire to allow this activity to also become still. Because I trusted the movement toward greater and greater peace, while in deepening states of very satisfying stillness, I could let go of mindfulness, of the functioning of the mind that clearly knows. Sometimes all that seemed to remain was awareness aware of itself.

Classic Buddhist teachings describe what I am calling "movements of mind" as mental activities or mental constructions. As I continued my practice, I heeded an intuition to let go of mental activities. At some point, when the mind was very quiet, I was surprised to "see" that everything that I could identify as a mental activity or mental construction ceased completely. Of course there was no seeing, as all inner and outer perception ceased as well. Even awareness disappeared. While this might seem to be a kind of death or a "nothing" that has no value, I found the experience to be life changing. It was more beautiful and satisfying than anything I had ever experienced before. More importantly, I felt changed.

Now I have a connection to a dimension of mind or of awareness that is unconstructed, with no movement or agitation in it. It is somewhat like remaining aware of a peaceful silence while simultaneously hearing the ring of a bell. The sense of the unconstructed became very important because it highlighted how everything else is constructed. Any understanding or sense of self is a construction of the mind—it has its role in life but it has no inherent existence. Any understanding of the world or even of Buddhist practice is a construct of the mind. Paradoxically, for practitioners, Buddhist teachings are constructs of mind that point beyond themselves.

While I do not know whether any of my deep meditation experiences qualify as enlightenment, they have inspired me to appreciate and respect the possibility of enlightenment as a radical and thoroughgoing freedom.

I now know that the Buddha's teaching that "Nothing whatsoever is worth clinging to" doesn't entail a loss or a diminishing of anything other than greed, hate, and delusion. "Nothing whatsoever is worth clinging to" points to the radiance of liberation, far beyond the practice of mindfulness.

THE ZEN OF VIPASSANA
A Dialogue Between Gil Fronsdal
and Max Erdstein

GIL FRONSDAL: Here in the West, many people participate in more than one tradition, finding them complementary. Both of us have been involved in both Soto Zen and in Vipassana practice at the Insight Meditation Society, at Spirit Rock, and in Burma. I started with Soto Zen at the San Francisco Zen Center in 1975, when I was twenty-one. I would have found it harder to do Vipassana practice, especially in Asia, without the foundation of having first done Soto Zen. As one of the new generation of teachers coming on, Max, how has that been for you?

MAX ERDSTEIN: My experience tracks yours in some ways but is also shaped by your experience, since you were my first Buddhist teacher. In 1996, when I was eighteen years old, I learned Mindfulness-Based Stress Reduction from a book in order to deal with a health problem and had a positive experience with meditation. But after that, my practice was dormant until I met you in 1999 and, at twenty-one years old, began sitting with your group in Palo Alto.

I agree that Zen practice can be an excellent foundation for doing more intensive Vipassana. But at age twenty-one I wouldn't have been ready to start with Zen—it seemed too religious for my taste, with its robes and rituals. I entered through the doorway of your group, rooted in the Western Insight scene, which doesn't use as many of the Asian outer forms. Then I heard you talk about your experience with Zen, and you mentioned Suzuki Roshi. That led me to Tassajara and the San Francisco Zen Center, which offered community, people my age I could practice with and even live with. I felt very held by that. Some years later, I returned to Vipassana and the

Insight tradition, which offered intensive residential experiences that were possible for people living in the world to plug into.

GF: It's instructive to look at the overlaps and contrasts between zazen and vipassana. To me the core aspect of the two practices is actually different. It has to do with a view of the purpose of religious life and what it means to be human.

In Zen, this world we live in is the place of awakening and freedom. Freedom is not something that you have to work toward attaining. It is rather something you allow to be expressed through you. It is already here. So zazen practice is more of an expression of Buddhahood.

It came as a big surprise to me that in Vipassana, you are looking at how the mind works. Investigation takes a huge priority that is not prominent in Zen.

ME: Yes, absolutely. After having sat with your group in the Insight tradition for a few years, I was surprised going to Tassajara as a summer student. I was hoping for deep concentration and instructions or koans. Instead, they said, "You always step with this foot, and sit this way, and put your hands like this. Make sure you have a straight back." And then the bell would ring. *Wait, what are we supposed to do while we are sitting here?* No one would answer the question.

I was a student at Stanford, and then I worked at Google, and I was very much in that "if you have something to do, do it well" mode. So Zen practice was a mystery. But in a way, not having instruction was liberating, precisely because I couldn't figure "it" out—"it" was outside the realm of doing it right or doing it wrong. Periods of zazen somehow felt more restful than periods of what I understood to be vipassana, where there were so many instructions and possible things one could do. *Do I focus on the breath here or here? Or maybe not focus on the breath?* Whereas zazen seemed so simple.

GF: Another way I benefitted from Zen training was that it taught me discipline—which helped me when I started with Vipassana in Thailand, where mostly I practiced alone. I was given a little cottage in the woods in which to do all my meditation. Through this solitary practice I realized that in Zen the discipline had come from the community practicing together. With Vipassana, I had to discover the inner discipline to keep me going.

ME: My first residential Vipassana retreat was a month-long retreat at Spirit Rock. I remember telling Guy Armstrong, a teacher I was interviewing with, how guilty I felt about staying up late to meditate. I wanted to keep the momentum going but then I was too sleepy to wake up for the first sitting.

In Zen, sittings aren't optional. The bell rings and you go to the meditation hall, and if you don't go, someone comes and knocks on your door. Often there will be a little trail of students, of yogis, whom the zendo manager is bringing in, who overslept.

But at Spirit Rock, Guy said something like, "What's so great about the early morning sitting?" That was a revelation for me. In Zen, you harmonize with the group and let go of your own preferences, habits, and conditioning. In contrast, the Vipassana retreat gave me a chance to discover how to develop practice for myself in a way that would be in harmony with the retreat but also with my own tempo and rhythm.

GF: The relationship between the teacher and student in Zen is also different from that in the Vipassana world. When I was in Asia with Sayadaw U Pandita, he was only interested in my meditation. Whereas at the San Francisco Zen Center, conversations with the teachers would be about all aspects of your life, work, or relationships. I think it's very valuable to be seen as a whole rather than only by one's meditation practice.

ME: I totally agree. At Zen Center you actually live with the teachers, so you see them as a whole too. The teaching is not only in talks and in interviews; it's how the teachers move, how they walk, their presence. When you're so close and intimate, it's more difficult to idealize the teacher. You see how the teachers deal with their own difficulties, which is very valuable for a student to see. Whereas at Spirit Rock, if someone is just seeing a teacher up on the teaching platform and for formal interviews, there may not be a chance to experience the teacher's whole being.

GF: Some of the important experiences I had with my Zen teachers involved working side-by-side doing manual labor at the monastery or in the garden. Just working together planting lettuce seedlings in the garden was a kind of teaching.

ME: Working at Tassajara, I found that we absorbed teachings through the body, not through the thinking mind. It was a physical kind of intelligence. Then hopefully that bodily intelligence informed other aspects of our lives.

GF: It's often said that Zen training is training for the body more than the mind.

ME: You can see that in the Dharma talks at a Zen center too. The Dharma expresses itself in the moment. There is a feeling that *each moment is it*, it's not somewhere other than here. That's a beautiful aspect of Zen.

GF: Yes, in Zen, *how* you are when you give the talk is more important than what you say. The *how* is that you are somehow manifesting your practice so some kind of truth about human nature gets expressed *through* you. You're being the Dharma—free of greed, hatred, and delusion—rather than talking about the Dharma.

In my Zen training, I learned the tremendous value of everyday practice. We practice in how we eat. We practice in how we take a shower. The same kind of presence, the same expression of truth that we had in zazen, is something we tried to actualize in every ordinary activity. So there wasn't this hard separation between the practice on the cushion and off the cushion.

ME: Yes, there is an integration that's built into Zen practice—a way of constantly sitting and then getting up off the cushion and doing things and coming back and getting up. There are multiple sittings a day at Zen centers; someone can sit, leave for work, then come back and sit again after work. That kind of support is a real gift. If meditation is only retreat practice, perhaps something is out of balance. In my teaching, I'd like to offer a balance of both: support for intensive retreats and also a lot of support for daily life practice.

GF: I've been watching the trends in what's taught as Vipassana in the West. There were times when the Burmese Mahasi approach was the main trend; it could be dualistic and striving and goal-oriented in a way that led some people to practice with a lot tension. Then some Vipassana teachers studied the nondual practices of Advaita and Dzogchen, where there was an emphasis on realizing freedom here and now. Over the years, the trends go one way or the other, I think in an effort to find a balanced approach between practicing hard and being relaxed.

So Max, now that you're a Vipassana teacher, what's the main legacy of your Zen training?

ME: As you said earlier, Zen emphasizes that the practice and the goal aren't two different things. Funny enough, I needed intensive Vipassana practice to clearly see this. When the mind is allowed to settle deeply, the need for goals drops away on its own. I cherish the immediacy and poetry of Zen and the simplicity, clarity, and pragmatism of Vipassana. Understood as skillful means, Zen and Vipassana are not really much different at all.

GF: In intensive Zen training I learned a lot about bringing myself wholeheartedly into the practice. In intensive Vipassana retreats I've come to a very simple understanding of the Dharma as a practice that frees us from suffering. I find it so satisfying to have a religious practice that's free of religion, free of abstract metaphysics and philosophical ideas. It feels liberating to have a wholehearted and direct way to address suffering. Once you're free of suffering, everything else takes care of itself.

8. SOLITUDE

ON MINDFULNESS IN THE ARTS

Norman Fischer

SOLITUDE

for Mei-mei Berssenbrugge

Plants are dreaming of me there's distance in their dream at whose
    vanishing point my
dream meets theirs which effects a melding in consciousness so that
    my thinking
of myself is a plant's thinking of a plant
In mythical realities I can hear them referring to things I've written
    in poems
but they are neither impressed nor unimpressed
Downstairs in someone's room I hear a cricket's song outside distant
    thunder as I said our lives are myths so ordinary things like
    meals or perceptions are symbolic
People can't communicate & that's painful yet people are close to
one another instinctually genetically, molecules of one flesh merging
mixing though pseudoidentities lost wander ponderous bodies
    tuned to identical frequencies Because they are equally beautiful
    people & plants merge usually in meals & death & become each
    other instinctually feeling support & love though there's only
    dreaming no thinking

so there's no illness, that's conceptual & based on a distorted
   projection into the space between molecules while in fact every
   living thing constantly
thrives in its own way
Still I stayed in bed today weakly at the same time I was transporting
myself into those plant-stems & those purple buds being visited by
earnest bees was I asleep or awake then?
Were the purple buds—now flowers fully opened—aware it was
   me dreaming them or was my dream more real than Mei-mei
   expected or deigned to describe in her text that's this I can hear
   the multiple buzz now, earnest
Again today I'm not feeling well a feeling that's good in the way it's
   not the feeling I'm used to that could meet an expectation of a
   certain kind of activity I might wish to be doing—I'm thinking—
   but I can't—
That's my memory jogging itself into action deciding what I think I
   might want
(wanting implying time passing from one state in me—as if I were—
   to the next)
No experience is one experience, first it's unregistered next it's a (false)
   memory then I'm making a puzzle out of it assign it a meaning
I'm assimilating you the various digesting consequences &
   reshaping them though there's really no agent as with each
   different leaf on that aspen tree there's repeating without
   repeating a finite number of possible shapes reiterated fractals
   nothing the same—not even the same
as itself (identity having come much later, like cuisine)
I keep thinking through something since I can never think
   through nothing (though I can think of that word)—anything is
   something a thing so thick and adamant facing
me expressive yet dumb like earth begging the question—so I become
   that thought's only fooling me in the meantime to be thinking me
   though I think I'm thinking it all this leaking out of me or
into me
from the day's clear or diffuse clouds from the hills gravel on the
   road large black beetle the bees downy woodpecker the sound

now of machinery there's a subtle vibration within (or as) silence
   that I feel as quiver in the hairs in my nostrils or small downy
   hairs on back
of neck alone in it there's a fuller sense of being as if it were actually
   something or anything combined with nothing—meaning silence
   or space—as I was saying that I remember participating in or
as
little white pieces of torn paper fluttering down indoors or snow
Self colors, covers that—I don't have to be naive this speaking there's
   nothing to explain when I'm here you must be too I noticed early
   on there was a difference in the room if someone were present or
   not that they'd draw me into an understandable world as a form
   of sharing to ease the anxiety that possibly there isn't anything
   filling in the immense hope with rainwater or tone of voice but
   there's no solitude otherwise
no social world nothing to speak about people always controversial
   with their opinions &
needs they're moved exactly as water flowing onward moves when
   redirected by rocks or banks or slowed by silt so there's only
   solitude yellow yarrow flowers cluster
in a bunch beyond them flagstone & a cherry tree little leaf
   movements twitch in slight breeze making a pattern speaking a
   language I don't know (a natural Morse code of short & longer
   movements) I stop to ponder
these movements my prelinguistic thought dances in tempo then
   body moves also
as these words my pen time isn't moving while I gingerly absorb
   these flavors my memory a story that never occurred except as I
   configure it my belief makes it so connection—nothing in itself—
   appears as a visual image I can't
identify any object but feel met & welcomed by space
Mirrors shine glitter reflect image at a point in time so
much now past—more than is future or present or past future
   present always
one quantity one tiny breach or gap into which suddenly a wave
   breaks drenches

recedes leaving again a gap for wave where there's feeling suddenly
    I see space opening I'm tired now so weary I think I hardly
    exist except as low hum of subvocal thought whisperingme into
    almostbeing this tiny point of feeling between us illuminating
me—or you—

***

This poem was written in July of 2014 when my wife Kathie and I were in residence for almost a month at Upaya Zen Center in Santa Fe, leading a short Zen practice period. During that time I was often ill (I had two abscessed teeth, causing me to run a fever much of the time, and I was on antibiotics). While we were there I had the rare chance to visit with an old friend, the great poet Mei-mei Berssenbrugge, to have dinner, hear her read her poems, and also to read, later, slowly and closely, her book *Hello, the Roses.*

Upaya is a beautiful temple, and the gardens at the Zen Center were full and vibrant in the hot and sunny July weather. In my mind, what most characterizes a Zen practice period is its sense of silence and timelessness. Days go by, always more or less the same, as if a single day. Each day punctuated by periods of zazen, so that one is constantly going back and forth to and from the zendo, many times each day. Walking paths become a metaphor for life, back and forth, back and forth, one long repetitive circular journey going nowhere.

I write all this to give a sense of the mood and surroundings out of which this poem comes. For me, a great poem is one that makes me write—that calls forth writing in me. *Hello, the Roses* forced me to write. The poem "Solitude" is the result.

Mei-mei's works in *Hello, the Roses* seem to be deep meditations on thinking and perceiving and being in the midst of natural environments—direct experiencing of living among, with, and as plants and animals. They come out of her unusual intelligence and sensitivity to the world. (Mei-mei speaks slowly and thoughtfully, in a quiet voice. Her body seems to register sensations and currents that most of us are insensitive to.) Writing my poem I felt in communion in some way, through the trance in which the words of the poem were inhabiting me, with Mei-mei, or rather, with the spirit she must have entered into, in her composition.

I wrote the poem without any idea of what it would be, where it would go. I had no idea I was trying to get across, no feeling I wanted to express. I simply wanted to inhabit the space of the poem I was writing for as long as that space was given to me. I say "I" "wanted," but it would be closer to true to say that the poem (which as yet did not exist) reached out in its inexistence, wanting me to inhabit it, to bring it into another order of being. At any rate, I was compelled to write what I was writing, even though I did not know what I was doing.

Perhaps this doesn't sound like "mindfulness." But I felt (without thinking this at the time) Mei-mei's mystic spaciousness, felt the silence and essential solitude of zazen and practice period, which seemed to rhyme with it, felt (and saw, heard, smelled, tasted, sensed in some way beyond the physical senses as well) the environment in which I was then situated.

My method was as usual: with pen in hand poised over notebook page, to listen for words that appear in my hand and ear, and then write them, one following another, phrase by phrase and line by line, each coaxing the next into physical recording. The process was, at it always is, immensely enjoyable and fully engaging. And a necessity for my well-being in a world that doesn't make sense to me, and which I find, the more seriously I take it, the more troubling.

Where do the words come from? I'm not sure. I have been speaking, listening to, reading, and writing within the English language my entire life, and the echo of all that (including the poetic tradition in which I am writing, postmodern innovative poetry, its sound and sensibility heard in thousands of texts) must give rise to the words that appear.

I wonder what is the condition of my mind when I am writing poems. Maybe it is something like what Freud called "evenly hovering attention." That is, my mind is open, poised in a sense—because I am long conditioned to snap into a specific kind of attention when I put a pen in my hand and open a notebook—to receive something. My attention is strong, but it isn't, as Freud indicates, focused. It's "hovering," and it is "evenly" hovering: open, searching, but not for any particular object or point. When words begin to come, the focus shifts to shapes and senses the words begin to suggest, and a more intentional mind takes over, yet one that is at the same time loose and relaxed, curious, not grasping at anything, still willing, at any point, to go elsewhere than where it is at the moment tending to go.

Or maybe my mind in writing exercises what Keats called "negative capability": the poet's capacity to completely let go and open into any space that appears, zero herself (hence "negative"), and therefore be fully ready to take in whatever else presents itself in the moment. Keats described this state in an often-quoted letter to his brothers: "At once it struck me what quality went to form a Man of Achievement, especially in Literature, and which Shakespeare possessed so enormously—I mean Negative Capability, that is, when a man is capable of being in uncertainties, mysteries, doubts, without any irritable reaching after fact and reason."

Another way of describing my mind when I am writing poems might be that in the moment of composition I practice what Dogen calls "thinking not-thinking, the essential art of zazen." By this he means, as I understand (and have practiced), that there may be thinking coming and going but the thinking is free and open, not driven by desire associated with self and its productions and needs. The thinking just comes and goes without direction or goal.

In this sense, my practice of poetry, like my practice of zazen, affords me a chance to forget about myself and simply float in language, feeling, thought, with an even and open sense.

(In all of this I am talking about the primary experience of initial composition. I always go back to poems later, after I have forgotten the initial feeling, and the poem seems then foreign to me, to shape, alter, cut, or add, in a more deliberate way.)

Zen is inspired by the emptiness teachings, which insist, elaborately and repetitively, that there isn't anything actually, that everything that seems to be what it is isn't, that all phenomena are evanescent, ungraspable, essentially dreamlike. So in Zen mindfulness is of necessity improvisational, open to surprise and accident.

Reality, it would seem, does not go according to previously determined plan or conform to a set of agreed-upon norms. For Zen—as for Buddhism in general—the problem, the ultimate oppressor, is self—that which identifies with predetermined plans and deeply held norms. Self that's socially conditioned, a product of its place, time, and situation. Self is suffering. Liberation is liberation from self. In terms of poetry, liberation would be liberation from self into the poem.

The recent history of art is full of enthusiasm for this sort of thing. Early in the twentieth century the great jazz musicians invented a form that depended on moment-by-moment improvisation. Being immersed formally in the moment perhaps served to liberate them from the suffering of their daily lives. The cult of immediacy they invented soon spread to all the other arts—the value of improvising and "authenticity" in the moment of composition has probably been the dominant ideology in art of the last hundred years or so.

There's no doubt that my lifelong practice of zazen has helped me as a poet. Before I practiced zazen I was trying to express myself and my ideas in my writing, and I was trying to write well, to achieve something of worth and note. I was very bad at this. Mostly because, as a young man, my sense of self was fairly crude and unconscious and constantly got in my way. I spent a decade or so of tortured apprenticeship, during which I wrote a great deal of bad material that was difficult to produce and that made me miserable. When I began to devote myself to zazen almost out of desperation I found eventually that I could enjoy writing, forget myself, and approach the work as adventure, surprise, *practice*, without having myself at stake.

It strikes me that this may be nearly the opposite of what is commonly thought of as "mindfulness practice"—the self's effort to pay attention to what is going on so as to clarify and to gain peace, insight, improved performance. Mindfulness is often presented as the best way to maximize the positive effects of "brain plasticity," cultivating certain kinds of attention, gently and effectively changing old habits of stress and reactivity.

I have no doubt mindfulness works—my personal experience bears this out. On the other hand, the very earnestness of the effort to practice mindfulness could work against itself—one could try too hard and therefore get in the way. Or, even avoiding this pitfall, too much emphasis on goal or technique could well narrow the creative possibilities.

Because of its emphasis on the emptiness teachings I referenced above, Zen seems not to promote mindfulness per se. The Zen approach seems to be simply to let go into openness and see what happens. In Zen, as in the arts, what drives this attitude, and what saves it from being mere sensation-seeking, or self-centered play, or laziness, is devotion and community.

Artists generally practice their art with tremendous devotion. They sacrifice a lot for it. And they appreciate one another for sharing this devotion to an endeavor that no one can appreciate as they do. (In the arts the only thing worse than failure, which brings economic suffering and nearly insurmountable difficulty in continuing, is success, which fosters self-repeating and creative atrophy.) In Zen it's the same: no one gets any credit or personal improvement from doing zazen, but those who are devoted to it appreciate one another for that very reason. It seems that whatever happiness or character improvement comes from the practice of the arts or Zen comes from devotion and community rather than through a more task-oriented cultivation of mental or emotional qualities.

One of my sons, Noah Fischer, is an artist / social activist deeply involved in an almost total critique of our contemporary social order, especially the arts. Listening to him, observing the lives of others, and thinking on my own, I can see the justice of his social critique. It's true that large institutions, floods of money, and the insane pace of life in our late capitalist moment make it nearly impossible for the average person to be a person—her soul is so swamped with the desires, dictates, and tough circumstances of daily living in a highly competitive, developed, and crowded world that it is difficult for her to find her footing as a human being. Even the successful are in crisis these days: how much more so those who are up against it socially and economically? If the situation is difficult for young men, for instance, it is even worse for young women, who now must be the best possible mothers while simultaneously besting men in career development and intellectual achievement.

What gets crippled in this frantic race toward greater and greater self-realization is any actual sense of simply being someone. Even the arts and meditation, as worldly pursuits, are part of the insanity. The market subsumes them too, so that all artists and spiritual teachers these days had better be at least as good at marketing as they are at the free and open production of their works.

Nevertheless, the moment of composition, the moment of meditation, can still be, and mostly still is, an open moment, a liberated moment.

One of my favorite lines in the Perfection of Wisdom in Eight Thousand Lines sutra (an emptiness sutra) is spoken by the gods, who have just been listening to the teaching of Subhuti, Buddha's great disciple, master of emptiness and friendliness, who has just told them that buddhas don't stand anywhere, because there isn't any place to stand. Yet they are well grounded in their placelessness. Hearing this, the gods say, "What the fairies talk and murmur, that we understand though mumbled. What Subhuti has just told us, that we do not understand."

Understanding, per se, whether it's understanding a poem, a person, or a moment of experience, is probably overrated. And worse, it might be oppressive. Openness, improvisation, letting go, immediacy, no-mind, presence, whatever you call it (and none of these words is quite right—and strictly speaking, there is no "it" referred to), might require that we suspend not only judgment but even understanding. That our capability be negative. Having no place to stand we can finally be well grounded.

9. PLASTIC, ZEN, AND MINDFULNESS

Janet Jiryu Abels

"Plastic bags" and "Zen"—in some sense, these two words might not spring to mind as inhabiting the same universe, but for me, plastic bags have become a powerful component of awakening through the practice of Zen mindfulness.

Ever since the documentary *An Inconvenient Truth* roused me from my ignorance about the damage humans are doing to the planet, I have been aware how very bad plastic bags are for the environment. They take roughly four hundred years to decompose, often end up in the world's oceans, and are made with oil. Like so many others who were educated by that 2006 documentary, soon after I saw it I began paying attention to how I carried home my groceries: trying to remember to bring reusable bags to the supermarket, and trying to remember to bring a small, fold-up bag whenever I went out for other items. I also began saving the plastic bags I did use and recycling them at the bins at my supermarket. Sporadically, I also washed out plastic sandwich bags, as my environmentally conscious daughter had urged me to do, and I even bought a wooden rack to dry them on.

However, I did not connect any of this to my Zen practice. I was simply doing "environmental stuff" that seemed unrelated to my years of practicing and teaching Zen.

This changed dramatically when, along with other members of our Still Mind Zendo sangha, I took part in the historic People's Climate March in New York City in September 2014. As anyone who was there can attest, it was an inspiring experience. More than 400,000 people from all walks of life came together to challenge the ignorance and greed of the individuals, corporations, and governments that are largely responsible for ruining our fragile ecosystem. For me, the most powerful part was to be gathered on one long, wide New York City block with members of so many local, national, and international faith-based communities.

Standing there with my fellow Buddhists and people of other faiths on West Fifty-Sixth Street for more than two hours, waiting to be able to move forward in the throngs of people, I realized for the first time that the climate crisis is a moral issue and that the Buddha's teaching of "Do no harm" applies to it. "Not killing" is the first of the Zen Buddhist grave precepts. What else were we humans doing but killing the earth?

And, for that matter, what else was *I* doing? That's when my nascent environmental mindfulness and my Zen practice came together. I knew that the way forward was the conscious application of the practice of mindfulness to my environmental awareness.

Mindfulness is one of the elements in the Buddha's Eightfold Path of Awakening, and for good reason. It is with mindfulness that meditation begins, and meditation is the heart of the Buddha Way. Mindfulness is an *upaya*—a skillful means for developing the staying power to remain grounded in, focused on, just this present moment. Zen teaches that the present moment—the now moment—is the only reality there is. Anything else is simply a construct of the human mind. "Somewhere else" is an idea; "the past" is an idea; "the future" is an idea. Even our thoughts about the present moment are ideas. But because the human mind creates such a vivid and seemingly unshakeable reality around these mind constructs, we believe that our thought-created ideas are real. They are not. Only through the practice of meditation, when the thought-creating mind is gradually stilled so that we can be in the present moment and not in our illusory "somewhere else," can we begin to see the reality in front of us *as it is* and not as we *think* it is. Receiving reality as it is allows us to see into what Zen calls its essential nature. Awakening to essential nature is called enlightenment, and when enlightenment happens, we see that nothing exists by itself. Everything exists only in a vast web of interbeing. So enlightenment inherently fosters an ecological awareness.

And it all begins with being in the present moment. But the present moment, the *now* moment, is an elusive entity because the present moment is continually in flux, continually changing, moving, never still. It can't be captured or described. It can only be experienced. Once experienced, it must be released, let go, so that one can be with the next *now* moment. All of which requires acute attention, focus, and... mindfulness. This is why the practice of mindfulness is an essential part of the Zen path of awakening, requiring a toolbox of various skillful mindfulness tools.

Plastic bags are now one of the mindfulness tools in my toolbox. They bring me to present-moment awareness because I am forced to pay attention whenever they are offered to me or when I find myself needing them.

Walking in the People's Climate March, another insight began to dawn on me. Although I'd started to be environmentally "mindful"—attuning to the plastic bag issue and engaging in other mindfulness practices such as turning off lights—I began to realize that I had been pinning the greed, hatred, and ignorance causing the climate crisis on people *out there*. I had conveniently left myself out. That the problem lay with *them*—the men and women of business and government, those seeking money and power—had been the comfortable storyline of my conditioned mind. I'd been seeing myself as just a helpless victim. I was saving plastic bags and turning off lights because of *their* greed.

When I realized that the climate crisis was also being caused by my own greed, hatred, and ignorance (what Zen calls the "Three Poisons"), my Zen practice and my environmental awareness came together even more. It was not just *them*; it was me. I was as much in the grasp of the Three Poisons as *they* were. Greed, hatred, and ignorance were a part of my life, too, and were influencing the daily choices I made as a consumer.

What had kept me from seeing this? I knew full well that nobody escapes the pull of these three ego-oriented human conditions, and I had striven to be aware of them as part of my Zen practice. Why had I not seen them operating in my eco-oriented life before? The inconvenient truth that began to dawn on me was this: *because it was so much easier.* I had donned the veil that we draw in front of our eyes when we see but we don't allow ourselves to *really* see. I turned away, unmindful, because it's so much easier to turn away. I blamed *them* because it's so much easier. Don't we do this so often with so many people and situations in our lives?

After the climate march, I became increasingly aware (and continue to be) that I was (am) a participant in the earth's suffering because of my unmindfulness of the causes of that suffering. Zen teaches that we must look at suffering directly and not turn away from it; that we must look at our addictions and not paper them over with easy excuses.

When we live in this new way, we see more clearly there is a path of release from suffering—our suffering as well as that of others, including the earth. It begins with a stronger commitment to mindfulness and deep meditation practice, through which we come to realize the delusory nature of our self-centered, mind-less habits. Eventually we come to realize that we are not separate entities but are interrelated with the ten thousand things, as Buddhism calls them, and the earth itself. We come to realize that our actions—even the smallest ones—affect the world, and we come to realize that mindful attention to everyday life choices is where the reversal of addictive destructive habits begins.

Ever since these insights following the march, I've striven to practice mindfulness in a much more focused way in relation to eco-practice. This has expanded mindfulness practice in other parts of my life as well, so that now I continually meet my ego-oriented selfishness, so easily masked before. I meet my desire for ease, comfort, and all those other products of consumer advertising that are so seductively easy to succumb to. I meet my choice of not having to succumb.

Not succumbing, though, requires attention, focus, and moment-to-moment awareness such as I'd never quite practiced before in my everyday life. Now I not only reject plastic bags in stores or recycle them when necessary, I also recycle sandwich bags, cling wrap, and plastic of all kinds. In doing so, I continue to be amazed by how much of our life is wrapped in plastic! I also practice turning off lights left on not just by me but by others. I try to use the air conditioner only if truly necessary. I put newspapers into the recycling basket at home, and every food carton that comes my way, and every scrap of paper. And when I do these things, when I make those extra efforts, I'm being present, I'm being in the moment, I'm being aware, and I'm being awake.

By doing these things, I've also come to realize that I'm connecting more deeply to the *people* whose lives are impacted by the environmental crisis. This *felt sense* body connection, which vividly brings to life my interrelatedness with all that is, has been the most life-giving product of my mindfulness eco-practice. When I turn off the water faucet instead of letting it run while I brush my teeth or wash the dishes, I connect with countless others in the world whose access to water is severely limited due to the droughts brought on by climate change. For me this is a moment of compassion, generated through the simple mindful act of turning off the faucet. It is visceral and powerful. When I mindfully leave no traces on my plate at the end of a meal or make an effort to not waste any food in my kitchen, I connect with countless others in the world who have little or no food because of poor crops, arid land, and the selfish choices of others— including myself. For me, this is another moment of compassion found in daily mindful attention to the items in my kitchen.

Such natural, deepening connection to others far away is, for me, the experience of Zen's compassionate "not-two": not just a truth grasped by the mind but an experience realized in the body and then acted upon. It is bringing me greater release from the poisons of my own greed, hatred, and ignorance because I'm now more aware, through my mindful eco-practice, not only how the earth but also how other people are impacted by my choices. This daily practice of compassion then opens me up to a life of greater balance and equanimity—the natural, ordinary, everyday Way of Zen.

It turns out that plastic bags and Zen don't inhabit separate universes at all. Neither do you or I.

10. DROWNING IN SUFFERING
MINDFUL FEMINISM FINDS ZEN LIBERATION

Grace Schireson

The most bracing Zen comment I ever heard came from Joko Beck: "If you don't take your practice off your cushion into your life, you are better off not meditating at all." We don't meditate and develop awareness in order to become good meditators; we develop mindful awareness to help the world.

This point was brought home to me particularly strongly on September 11, 2001, as I watched on television as New York City buildings crumbled. I realized that sharing this planet means that destructive thoughts, feelings, and actions, even those seemingly far away, actually exist and carry consequences in this present moment. 9/11 and its aftermath provoked questions about my responsibility to prevent harm in my community and further afield. Horrifically painful images continued to dominate the news, and as I watched and rewatched, the incidents became my trauma—my vicarious trauma. And even vicarious traumatization has the power to undermine a person's well-being or thwart a helper's ability to comfort family, clients, or students.

Despite my efforts to settle my mind, I continued to feel raw and aimless. Seeking a remedy for my distress and sadness, I scheduled a trip to Japan to spend seven days, the first week of November 2001, in a meditation retreat at Tofukuji monastery with my Japanese Rinzai Zen teacher, the late Fukushima Keido Roshi (1933–2011). I hoped a period of intense Zen koan practice in a seven-hundred-year-old Zen temple would help restore my equilibrium. Koan practice focuses the mind on a single nonrational expression; since the expression is impossible to grasp with thinking, deep mindful concentration arises as the thinking mind subsides. This quest to calm my mind turned out to be a long and round-about journey, and while it led to fulfilling an important purpose, the route was challenging and painful.

When I arrived at Tofukuji temple in Kyoto, I was granted a private interview with Fukushima Roshi. As always, he was warm and gracious. His first remark was an offer of condolences for the events of September 11. Fukushima Roshi had spent a year living in California and had visited universities in the United States every year for more than a decade. He was fond of Americans and made special efforts to welcome them to his temple. For years, he had allowed Western women (although not Japanese women) to sit with the training monks in the *sodo*, the monks' training hall. I am unaware of any other official Japanese training temple that allows women such accessibility—despite the fact that the founder of Japanese Soto Zen, Eihei Dogen Zenji, wrote an essay about the foolishness of Japanese Buddhism excluding women from its important sites: *Raihaitokuzui*, or "Attaining the Marrow." Yet the exclusion of women from practicing in the sodo at Eiheiji, the monastery Dogen Zenji founded, continues to this day.

As I watched my worrying, fretting mind, a stubborn question formed over and over again. Radical Islam's well-planned killings of random civilians had arisen in overwhelmingly male-dominated cultural contexts. Not only were women excluded from leadership in the radical groups at the time of 9/11, but beyond a certain age, many men in the larger societies had grown up separated from girls and women. There was a lack of acquaintance with women and feminine culture.

This absence of the feminine in the terrorist mentality bore an embarrassing likeness to traditional Buddhist practice, where women were still barred from practicing in well-established monasteries. I had never attempted to influence or interact with radical Islam, but what exactly was my responsibility to speak or act when I encountered discrimination against women at Tofukuji temple?

In the aftermath of September 11, I realized that speaking to the temple's abbot about Buddhism's discrimination against female practitioners was truly my responsibility. Observing the problem, silently making my peace with the prejudice, and continuing to participate: this was no longer an option. I remembered what Joko Beck had said about taking practice into your life. Mindfulness teaches we must start by being aware of conditions as they are, initially accepting them without judgment so we may see them clearly—but mindfulness without an appropriate response wastes an opportunity. The only thing necessary for the triumph of evil is for good women to do nothing.

Western women who came to practice with the young monks at Tofukuji were seated in their place in the sodo. As is usual in Japanese temples, seating arrangements reflected status and position. The Buddha himself had ranked monks and nuns not just by their seniority but also by gender: the most junior monk was senior to the most senior nun. The nuns' ordination and monthly ceremonies required the presence of monks, but the monks were not dependent on the nuns for ordination, supervision, or teaching. The Buddhist nuns' order was not only separate from but also unequal to that of the monks.

The rules for seating arrangement at Tofukuji displayed some of this old Buddhist order. The Tofukuji monks were ranked by their seniority and roles; next came other non-Japanese visiting Asian Buddhist monks, then all Western men, then all Western women. And there was no differentiation among ordained and lay Westerners. I noted how this differed from the Buddha's four communities (ordained men, ordained women, lay men, and lay women), but the slight seemed symbolic and didn't cause me much concern; I was grateful that Fukushima Roshi allowed Westerners and women to practice with his monks.

Consistent with the seating order, I often found myself last in line for my koan interview, or *dokusan*, with Fukushima Roshi. After a dozen sesshins and more than fifty dokusan interviews, I understood the protocol. I had been instructed that when I was last in line, I was to strike the bell twice to announce my upcoming interview, rather than once, as everyone who came before me did. In this way, the entire temple would know that the interviews were complete, and the next activity could be scheduled—lunch, service, or rest. Waiting for dokusan in last position was not a hardship; I appreciated that all of us waiting together were focused on penetrating our own koan, sitting in close quarters with respect, concentrated silence, and privacy.

But gender discrimination could have its effects even here. I was startled one time when, after I'd been practicing at Tofukuji for about ten years, a Western man who was a newcomer to the temple spoke to me as I silently awaited my turn. "You know y'all are the last one in dokusan? And you know we all are waiting in the zendo for you to finish your koan. So don't take too long in your interview, don't make us wait for you. Okay?" The fact that he had felt free to interrupt my concentration, and to disparage my efforts by treating my koan practice as just a nuisance to the rest of the sangha, consisting entirely of males, and that I should hurry along so as not to burden their practice, momentarily stunned me. I was so shocked by his intrusion, his entitlement, his disrespect for my practice, and his rudeness that all I could utter was "thank you," and bow. My gender and place in the line-up had made me vulnerable to this newcomer's contempt. After that encounter, but without referring to it directly, I questioned Fukushima Roshi about the fact that Westerners were not ranked by ordination or seniority, but by gender. He did not have much to say, and nothing changed in this regard at Tofukuji.

When I returned to the temple after the events of September 11, I left a gift and a card for Fukushima Roshi at the start of the silent retreat. In addition to describing my upset over the violent events, and expressing my gratitude for the opportunity to train at Tofukuji, in my note I commented on the discrimination in both radical Islam and in Buddhism: "Don't you think it is time for Buddhism to come out from behind its own veil regarding women?" I didn't discuss my note with anyone; I simply joined in meditation and koan practice with the rest of the monks. However, during Fukushima Roshi's lecture to the community a couple of days into the retreat, I received what I believed to be Fukushima Roshi's response to my question about Buddhist discrimination against women.

Once or twice a week, Fukushima Roshi offered a lecture at Tofukuji to the local community. Usually about twenty people, mostly women, would come for tea and the talk. During the talk, all of the monks and myself were on one side of the Buddha Hall, and all of the guests were on the other. We sat in rows facing our guests, and I had a clear view of many of the neighborhood women in attendance. They seemed to be interested and pleased that a woman, even a Western woman, was part of the training at the temple. They acknowledged me with their eyes and with small nods and smiles.

All of Fukushima Roshi's lectures were based on the teachings of the great Zen master Joshu (Ch., Zhaozhou; 778–897). On that particular day, several days after my request that Buddhism come out from behind the veil, Fukushima Roshi lectured on the story of a nun. When he introduced the story and mentioned the nun, I watched the female guests perk up, like flowers seeking the sun. I perked up too; I watched the women facing me, listening eagerly.

In the story, a nun asked Joshu, "I have a body with the five hindrances. How can I escape them?" Since the time of the Buddha, women were described as having this body with the five hindrances, which prevented them from becoming a buddha in their female lifetime. This is how Joshu answered her question about how she could awaken as a woman: "Pray that all of your oppressors are born in Heaven, and pray that you yourself drown eternally in a sea of hardships."

At this, all of the women, who just a few sentences earlier had sat up so bright and tall, physically caved in defeat. They hung their heads and looked deflated after hearing Joshu's practice instructions to this woman. Throughout the rest of Fukushima Roshi's lecture the women in the audience looked despondent. Was I watching, in this very moment, the weight of twenty-five hundred years of Buddhist discrimination against women impose its crushing effects?

I left the lecture, carrying my indignation on their behalf back to my cushion. I continued the meditation retreat in silence for another five days. During that time, I persisted with my formal koan practice, but I also remained mindful of Zen Master Joshu's words to the struggling nun, and the response of the Japanese women during the lecture. Were Joshu's words another expression of cultural oppression to women, even as they tried to manifest buddhahood? The wisdom of this particular Joshu teaching story seemed questionable at best and harmful at worst. I also worried that Fukushima Roshi had been insensitive to his local female supporters. Both mindfulness and Zen practice, after all, require we be aware of who and what is immediately in front of us.

At the end of the seven days of meditation, I had a private exit interview with Fukushima Roshi. After five days of concentrated practice, my anger and frustration had been replaced by determination. Perhaps this is one of the fruits that emerge when Zen and mindfulness meet. I referred to the story in Roshi's lecture, and then I said, "Zen Master Joshu was wrong about this." I expected Fukushima Roshi to find my statement, my placing myself in a position to critique Joshu, to be jarring.

Fukushima Roshi had been a Zen monk for fifty-four years at this point, and I suspect all those years practicing composure helped him not to drop his jaw in astonishment at my chutzpah. I watched him respond as carefully as I did in koan dokusan. After all, I had been ordained as a Zen priest for only three years. Fukushima Roshi believed Joshu was the greatest Zen master of all time, but he also believed that his students needed to express their practice freely and sincerely. Was I testing his limits on my Zen freedom?

Without expressing the least detectable amazement, Roshi accepted my challenge and asked, "What do you mean?" I felt his scrutiny underneath his inviting question. He smiled at me, as if to say, "Come on in," as a spider to a fly. My American Soto teacher, Sojun Mel Weitsman Roshi, had said about practice between teacher and disciple, "I'll turn you and you turn me." The Dharma is not written in stone; it is a conversation that is rooted in meditation, Dharma teachings, and human embodiment. Fukushima Roshi was encouraging and testing my embodiment with his own.

I continued. "A Zen master has a responsibility to correct what is unjust in his society or at least to acknowledge the injustice. Joshu needed to concede and deplore the discrimination against Buddhist women to which the nun referred. Without acknowledging this cultural prejudice, instead he asked her to drown in the suffering the unfairness caused her. He allowed this cultural bias to continue unchallenged, and therefore he reinforced it as a given."

Fukushima Roshi nodded and seemed unperturbed. He answered, "Through this difficult practice, the nun can completely accept her suffering if she follows Joshu's advice. This nun could find her freedom—her freedom to manifest Zen mind no matter how difficult or unfair the circumstances. Zen is about finding your freedom."

I agreed that difficulty was an important element of practice and said, "The thing is, women have had many such difficulties over many centuries. These hardships are truly good for practice. But why should women get all of these advantages? If such hardships are so good for practice, so effective for finding freedom, why do women get so many of the extra difficulties? It isn't fair. Men should have the same opportunities to practice with these kinds of hardships that have been so helpful to women."

Fukushima Roshi chuckled at my logic and brought up a story where two monks give similar answers and the teacher says, "The first monk's head is white, the second monk's head is black." "Do you know that story?" he asked. "Yes, I know the story. The verse that goes with it says 'White head, black head, capable heirs of the house.' I wonder if you are trying to talk to me about separate but equal. We know something about that in the United States. Do you want to talk about how that worked in my country?"

Now, Fukushima Roshi's face showed a trace of concern. "Oh, you mean civil rights in America?" I nodded, "Yes." Fukushima Roshi responded, "But the Buddha's teaching is a teaching of equality." And I agreed: "Yes, of course, that is why I am here. Manifesting equality is what Buddha taught and what we do. But you can't say that the practice of the most senior nun being junior to the most junior monk is an example of equality. That isn't right, is it?"

Fukushima shook his head in agreement. "No, it is not right," he said. Fukushima Roshi and I had arrived together at an understanding, and I imagined he might have been making a mental note to himself: "This business about women and Buddhism is a tricky matter. Discussing women in Buddhism with a feminist priest from Berkeley could prove challenging." What he said out loud was "I will be sending you home with several more koan." I inferred from this last assertion that no matter what the wisdom was about women in Buddhism, and no matter how accepting he was of my challenge, he was the teacher from whom I would need to receive koan training, and I would remain his student in that relationship, as I did for the rest of his teaching life.

I left the temple to return to America, satisfied to have put my practice to use on behalf of the women potentially disappointed by Joshu's words and Fukushima Roshi's commentary. Using the strength and calmness developed on the cushion, along with the honesty of my willing teacher, I felt I had fulfilled my vow to be accountable. Mindful awareness, sharply focused by the koan practice, became alive in the dialogue with my teacher. The engagement of mindfulness is one way we can help to change the world we meet.

And there may have been other consequences. Even though the seating and the protocol did not change at the temple, exceptions were made when I brought my male students to the temple for zazen. The monks in the sodo allowed me to sit in a more senior position in relation to my own male students. More importantly, in an interview conducted and transcribed in the 2003 book about Fukushima Roshi's calligraphy, *Zen No Sho*, the editor, Professor Jason Wirth, recorded these words of Fukushima Roshi as having been expressed in November 2001:

> [The] United States is making a very important advance on traditional Buddhism in the case of women. For the first time, women and men are represented in Buddhism in equal numbers, and compared to other Buddhist traditions, women are treated in American Buddhism in a kind of ideal and democratic way. I think this is an important advance for women.[1]

When I found this quote I couldn't help but think that when he was asked about American Zen by Professor Wirth in Kyoto, he reflected on our conversation earlier in that month. Further ripples from our conversation might have been heard when he spoke to my own students visiting Tofukuji in 2007. He said, "The most important change in American Zen is the equality of women Zen masters. You have many female Zen masters in America, and we only have a few in Japan. This is a real advantage."

An early Chinese Zen master, Zongmi (780–841), described the interaction of the Dharma and the Zen practitioner's mind in this way:

To use the teachings of the sage as a luminous mirror,
in which to see one's own mind reflected,
And to use one's own mind as a lamp of wisdom,
with which to illumine the profound meaning of the scriptures.

Zongmi described an essential and dynamic interaction of teacher, Dharma, and practitioner. The process of becoming aware, becoming awakened, requires both the Dharma teachings and the mind of a sage. Once the practitioner's mind has been reflected in the Dharma's luminous mirror, it can receive this light. The practitioner's mind and the actions that flow from it may then become a lamp that can illumine the scriptures and take the teaching to a more profound level.

This engaged relationship, between mindful sages and mindful students, maintains the Dharma's vitality, and it is also how the student makes the Dharma her own, on and off the cushion. Your mindfulness needs to illumine this very life for your own sake and for the sake of the flowering of the Dharma.

Did my conversation with Fukushima Roshi, created by my own vow and practice, influence his comments to Professor Wirth a week later? Maybe, but Fukushima Roshi and I never discussed it. What was and is important to me was my decision to take my mindfulness practice off the cushion and into my life. One may never see or know just what the consequences will be, but such actions are ripples, visible or invisible, moving in all directions to extend illumination to the Dharma and to the lives of practitioners, born and to be born.

11. A BITE OF THE UNIVERSE

Sojun Mel Weitsman

When I was asked to write this article I wondered what I could possibly say about mindfulness that had not been wonderfully expressed by every Buddhist teacher from the time of Shakyamuni up until now. Then early this afternoon, while I was putting together an avocado sandwich as I have done many times before, and wondering how I could respond to Bob's request, I remembered one time thinking about the number of ingredients and the number of moves it takes to make this sandwich, where all these different ingredients come from, and the innumerable efforts it takes to grow and deliver them.

As we know, the way of practice is to eat just enough to get by without being seduced by the pleasure. But I just can't ignore the wonderful taste of a good oily, ripe avocado. So what do I do? I walk two blocks to the Monterey produce market, aware of my steps, my breath, and my posture. I pick out a ripe avocado (from California), walk over to the breads and pick up a loaf of Vital Vittles whole-wheat sesame made on San Pablo Avenue. I walk to the counter and exchange a piece of paper for that loaf of bread and walk mindfully home.

I turn the door handle, walk through the door and over to the kitchen.

I put the bread on the counter. I walk to the refrigerator, open it, take out the mustard (from France), and put it on the counter along with a lemon from our tree. I close the refrigerator and walk out to the garden to pick a tomato and some lettuce leaves (sometimes we'll buy this produce at the store), walk back into the kitchen and line up the ingredients. I get a knife from the drawer and take two pieces of bread out of the package; open the mustard jar, scoop some out, and spread it on the bread; cut the avocado in two, scoop one half and spread it on the bread; reach for the salt and shake some on; then squeeze the lemon, slice the tomato, put the lettuce on, and put the other piece of bread on top.

Then I put the top of the jar on the mustard, tie up the bread, cover the tomato and the other half of the avocado with Glad Wrap, open the refrigerator, and put them away one by one. But these are just the obvious steps. It's easy to be mindful here because I am focused on making something delicious, and if my mind wanders it's easy to come back to the subject at hand.

When I take that walk to the store, I like to feel that the floor or the sidewalk is also walking me. The terrain is teaching me how to walk on it if I pay attention. The avocado is teaching me how to hold it when I slice it and scoop it; so is the knife and the shape of the mustard jar, one hand holding and one hand turning the cover. All these many moves and more are integrating and balancing this variety of ingredients each with its own history, family, environment, texture, flavor, shape, and compatibility. Each thing I encounter is letting me know how to dance or flow with it. Establishing a rhythm is important. If I move too fast tension builds up. If I move too slowly it becomes tedious.

I say it is an avocado sandwich because in the complement of ingredients the avocado appears so prominently. But I could just as easily call it a mustard sandwich with avocado, or a lettuce sandwich with mustard and tomato and avocado. I have always liked the Catholic communal sacrament of the wafer and the wine as partaking of the flesh and blood of the deity. Our formal Zendo Oryoki meals have a similar quality for me. Whatever we eat is the flesh and blood of Buddha.

Finally I bow, and with two hands, hold this vibrant, living concoction to my mouth and take a delicious bite of the universe. Mindful of paying back mother nature for such providence, anything left over goes back to nourish the earth in return. From the first time that I turned over the soil many years ago and felt the warmth of the sun on the bottom of my feet I have had a deep reverence for the earth. We are admonished to walk lightly, leaving no trace, like the path of the bird or the fish. But with awareness that we and the earth and its creatures are two, yet one, with gratitude, we have a bond of mutual nourishment.

My teacher Suzuki Roshi said that his was not a mindfulness or concentration practice. Someone asked if he chewed his brown rice one hundred times with each bite. He said that if he did that he would not enjoy his meal. But mindfulness was always there; it was not a matter of counting to a certain number.

I think of two aspects of mindfulness: mindfulness of the self, and mindfulness of forgetting the self and doing what we can for others. One is focusing inward and the other focusing outward. Although Suzuki Roshi may not have chewed his rice one hundred times, we were always impressed by his thoroughness. His own self-assessment was that he was always forgetful. But he did teach us to be mindful and to respect our surroundings with simple, practical instructions:

Don't scrape the chair across the floor.
A table is not a chair.
Hold the teacup with both hands.
Kill just one bird with one stone.
Let the bluejay's squawk come right into your heart.
Your friend is more than just your friend
—just step back and settle down in the center of it all for the sake of
    all beings.

EPILOGUE

IS MINDFULNESS BUDDHIST?
(AND WHY IT MATTERS)

Robert H. Sharf

INTRODUCTION

In a chapter in an edited volume on the role of culture in depression, Gananath Obeyesekere begins by quoting from Brown and Harris's influential 1978 study on the social origins of depression in women:

> The immediate response to loss of an important source of positive value is likely to be a sense of hopelessness, accompanied by a gamut of feelings, ranging from distress, depression, and shame to anger. Feelings of hopelessness will not always be restricted to the provoking incident—large or small. It may lead to thoughts about the hopelessness of one's life in general. It is such generalization of hopelessness that we believe forms the central core of depressive disorder.[1]

To this Obeyesekere responds:

> This statement sounds strange to me, a Buddhist, for if it was placed in the context of Sri Lanka, I would say that we are not dealing with a depressive but a good Buddhist. The Buddhist would take one further step in generalization: it is not simply the general hopelessness

of one's own lot; that hopelessness lies in the nature of the world, and salvation lies in understanding and overcoming that hopelessness.[2]

One might want to quibble with Obeyesekere; one might demand more evidence—both psychological and ethnographic—for the similarities he sees between good Sri Lankan Buddhists and American depressives. Do Sri Lankan Buddhists really aspire to a state that we would associate with depression? Or is the very idea of depression so culturally and historically constructed as to mitigate its cross-cultural utility? However one parses these issues, on purely *doctrinal* grounds Obeyesekere has a point: early Buddhist sutras in general, and Theravāda teachings in particular, hold that (1) to live is to suffer, (2) the only genuine remedy to suffering is escape from *samsara* (the phenomenal world) altogether, and (3) escape requires, among other things, abandoning hope that happiness in this world is possible.

If one has any doubts, consider the advanced stages of insight described in the *Path of Purification* (*Visuddhimagga*), an authoritative Pali compendium composed by the fifth-century monk Buddhaghosa in Sri Lanka. After an exhaustive account of the various practices and meditative states discussed in the scriptures, Buddhaghosa turns to the ascending "stages of insight" that immediately precede the attainment of liberation. The eight stages of insight include "knowledge of dissolution," "knowledge of appearance as terror," and "knowledge of danger," and Buddhaghosa resorts to vivid similes to capture the affective tone that accompanies these rarefied states. One of the most harrowing is found in the description of "knowledge of appearance as terror":

A woman's three sons had offended against the king, it seems. The king ordered their heads to be cut off. She went with her sons to the place of their execution. When they had cut off the eldest one's head, they set about cutting off the middle one's head. Seeing the eldest one's head already cut off and the middle one's head being cut off, she gave up hope for the youngest, thinking, "He too will fare like them." Now, the meditator's seeing the cessation of past formations is like the woman's seeing the eldest son's head cut off. His seeing the cessation of those present is like her seeing the middle one's head being cut off. His seeing the cessation of those in the future, thinking, "Formations to be generated in the future will cease too," is like her giving up hope for the youngest son, thinking, "He too will fare like them." When he sees in this way, knowledge of appearance as terror arises in him at that stage.[3]

In other words, the emotional valence of this advanced stage of insight is likened to that of a mother being forced to witness the execution of all three of her sons. Could one imagine a more disturbing image of human anguish? Yet, according to Theravāda teachings, it is necessary to experience such despair—to confront the unmitigated horror of sentient existence—so as to acquire the resolve necessary to abandon the last vestiges of attachment to things of this world. Obeyesekere would seem to have a point: states akin to what we identify as "depression" would seem to be valorized, if only for the insight they engender, on the Buddhist path.

Yet today Buddhist insight is touted as the very antithesis of depression. Rather than cultivating a desire to abandon the world, Buddhism is seen as a science of happiness—a way of easing the pain of existence.[4] Buddhist practice is reduced to meditation, and meditation, in turn, is reduced to mindfulness, which is touted as a therapeutic practice that leads to an emotionally fulfilling and rewarding life. Mindfulness is promoted as a cure-all for anxiety and affective disorders including posttraumatic stress, for alcoholism and drug dependency, for attention-deficit disorder, for antisocial and criminal behavior, and for the commonplace debilitating stresses of modern urban life.

BUDDHIST MODERNISM AND THE RHETORIC OF BARE ATTENTION

The notion that Buddhism is a rational, empirical, and therapeutically oriented tradition compatible with modern science is one of the characteristic features of "Buddhist modernism" (sometimes known as "Protestant Buddhism"), an approach to Buddhism that evolved out of a complex intellectual exchange between Asia and the West that took place over the last 150 years or so. As there is now a robust literature on this subject, there is little need to rehearse it here.[5] My focus is on the particular practice most characteristic of Buddhist modernism, namely, "mindfulness" (Pali: *sati*, Sanskrit: *smṛti*), and more specifically, the interpretation of mindfulness as "bare attention" or "present-centered awareness," by which is meant a sort of nonjudgmental, nondiscursive attending to the here-and-now.

Scholars have argued that the widespread understanding of mindfulness as bare attention has its roots in the Theravāda meditation revival of the twentieth century, a movement that drew its authority, if not its content, from the two recensions of the *Scripture on Establishing Mindfulness* (*Satipaṭṭhāna Sutta*),[6] as well as Buddhaghosa's *Path of Purification* (*Visuddhimagga*), and a few other Pali sources. The specific techniques that came to dominate the *Satipaṭṭhāna* or *Vipassana* ("insight") movement, as it came to be known, were developed by a handful of Burmese teachers in the lineages of Ledi Sayādaw (U Nyanadaza, 1846/7–1923) and Mingun Sayādaw (U Nārada, 1869–1955).[7] Mingun's disciple Mahāsi Sayādaw (1904–82) developed the technique that is best known today, in which the practitioner is trained to focus on whatever sensory object arises in the moment-to-moment flow of consciousness. Mahāsi designed this method with laypersons in mind, including those with little or no prior exposure to Buddhist doctrine or liturgical practice.[8] Perhaps most radical was Mahāsi's claim that the cultivation of liberating insight did not require advanced skill in concentration (*samatha*) or the experience of absorption (*jhāna*). Instead, Mahāsi placed emphasis on the notion of sati, understood as the moment-to-moment, lucid, nonreactive, nonjudgmental awareness of whatever appears to consciousness. One of Mahāsi's most influential students, the German born monk Nyanaponika Thera (Siegmund Feniger, 1901–1994), coined the term "bare attention" for this mental faculty, and this rubric took hold through his popular 1954 book *The Heart of Buddhist Meditation*.[9]

Western Buddhist enthusiasts may have a hard time appreciating just how radical Mahāsi's method was in its day. Designed to be accessible to laypersons, it did not require familiarity with Buddhist philosophy or literature, most notably with the scholastic literature known as *abhidhamma*. (Traditional forms of Theravāda meditation required proficiency in the categories and methods of *abhidhamma* analysis.) It also did not require renunciation of lay life, and it could be taught in a relatively short period of time in a retreat format. All this made it easy to export, and it has been influential not only in the Southeast Asian Theravāda world, but also among modern Tibetan, Chinese, Korean, Japanese, and Vietnamese religious reformers. By the end of the twentieth century, Mahāsi's approach to mindfulness, understood as "bare attention" and "living in the here and now," had emerged as one of the foundations of Buddhist modernism—an approach to Buddhism that cut across geographical, cultural, sectarian, and social boundaries.[10]

The meaning of the term "mindfulness" is presumed by many to be self-evident, and thus modern exponents of mindfulness meditation may see little need to explore the intellectual history of the concept in Buddhism.[11] "Mindfulness" is a translation of the Sanskrit smṛti (Pali: sati), a term that originally meant "to remember," "to recollect," "to bear in mind." Its religious significance is sometimes traced to the Vedic emphasis on setting to memory the authoritative teachings of the tradition. The Pali term sati retains this sense of "remembering" in the Nikāyas (the scriptures attributed to the Buddha in the Theravāda school): "And what, bhikkhus, is the faculty of sati? Here, bhikkhus, the noble disciple has sati, he is endowed with perfect sati and intellect, he is one who remembers, who recollects what was done and said long before."[12] Moreover, the faculties of recollection and reflection were unarguably central to a variety of classical practices associated with smṛti, including buddhānusmṛti or "recollection of the Buddha," which typically involves some combination of recalling the characteristics of the Buddha, visualizing him, and chanting his name.

Even in the Satipaṭṭhāna Sutta, the term sati retains a sense of "recollecting" or "bearing in mind." Specifically, sati involves bearing in mind the virtuous dharmas so as to properly apprehend, from moment to moment, the true nature of phenomena. At least this is the explanation found in early Pali exegetical works such as the Milindapañha[13] and the commentaries of Buddhaghosa.[14] Rupert Gethin (The Buddhist Path to Awakening), who has undertaken a careful analysis of such passages, notes that sati cannot refer to "remembering" in any simple sense, since memories are, as Buddhists are quick to acknowledge, subject to distortion. Rather, sati

> should be understood as what allows awareness of the full range and extent of dhammas; sati is an awareness of things in relation to things,

and hence an awareness of their relative value. Applied to the *sati-paṭṭhānas*, presumably what this means is that sati is what causes the practitioner of yoga to "remember" that any feeling he may experience exists in relation to a whole variety or world of feelings that may be skillful or unskillful, with faults or faultless, relatively inferior or refined, dark or pure.[15]

In short, there is little "bare" about the faculty of sati, since it entails, among other things, the proper discrimination of the moral valence of phenomena as they arise.[16]

CRITIQUES OF MINDFULNESS AS BARE ATTENTION

There are, in addition, philosophical objections to construing sati as bare attention. The popular understanding of bare attention presumes that it is possible to disaggregate prereflective sensations (what contemporary philosophers sometimes refer to as "raw feels" or *qualia*) from perceptual experience writ large. In other words, there is an assumption that our recognition of and response to an object is logically and/or temporally preceded by an unconstructed or "pure" impression of said object that can be rendered, at least with mental training, available to conscious experience. Mindfulness practice is then a means to quiet the ongoing chatter of the mind and to keep to the "bare registering of the facts observed."

Superficially, this notion of mindfulness as bare attention would seem tied to a view of the mind as a sort of *tabula rasa* or clear mirror that passively registers raw sensations prior to any recognition, judgment, or response. The notion of a conscious state devoid of conceptualization or discrimination is not unknown to Buddhist exegetes; indeed, later Buddhist philosophers associated with *pramāṇa* (logic) and *yogācāra* (mental construction) systems posit a "nonconceptual cognition" (*nirvikalpajñāna*) that operates by means of "direct perception" (*pratyakṣajñāna*), and these authors use the imagery of the mirror to illustrate the relationship between pure mind and defiled object. This state is sometimes understood as preceding (or undergirding) the arising of conceptualization, or as an advanced stage of attainment tantamount to awakening.[17] But while the notion of nonconceptual cognition became important in some *yogācāra* systems (not to mention Tibetan Dzogchen), it remained at odds with the Theravāda analysis of mind and perception. In Theravāda abhidharma, consciousness and the object of consciousness emerge codependently and are hence phenomenologically inextricable. That is to say, the objects of experience appear not upon a preexistent *tabula rasa*, but rather within a cognitive matrix that includes affective and discursive dispositions occasioned by one's past activity (*karma*).[18] The elimination of these attendant dispositions does not yield "nonconceptual awareness" so much as the cessation of consciousness itself.[19] Arguing along similar lines, Paul Griffiths suggests that the closest thing to a state of unconstructed or pure experience in classical Indian Buddhist literature is *nirodhasamāpatti*—a condition in which both objects *and* conscious experience cease altogether.[20] In such a framework, it seems misleading to construe *any* mode of attention or perception as "bare." The psychological model behind Nyanaponika's understanding of sati as bare attention may owe more to internalist and empiricist epistemologies than it owes to early Buddhist or traditional Theravāda formulations.[21]

Given the ambiguities surrounding sati, it is not surprising that the Mahāsi method quickly came under fire from a number of quarters, including both Theravāda traditionalists in Southeast Asia and practitioners and scholars in the West. Critics object to (1) Mahāsi's devaluation of concentration techniques leading to absorption (Pali: *jhāna*); (2) claims that practitioners of the Mahāsi method are able to attain advanced stages of the path, including the four stages of enlightenment (Pali: *ariya-magga*), in remarkably short periods of time; and (3) the ethics of rendering *sati* as bare attention, which would seem to devalue or neglect the importance of ethical judgment.[22]

In my own work on the roots of the Zen (Chinese: Chan) tradition in eighth-century China, I found that certain early Zen teachers seem to have turned away from traditional forms of meditation—repentance practices, meditations on corpses and the impurity of the body, and so on—in favor of instructing their disciples to simply set aside all distinctions and conceptualizations, and allow the mind to come to rest in the flow of the here-and-now.[23] It may not be a coincidence that the teachers who advocated this new style of practice were also those who had garnered a sizable lay audience, an audience that presumably had little interest in monastic renunciation and little background in Buddhist doctrine. So these early Zen techniques, which went under the rubrics of "viewing mind" (kanxin), "discerning mind" (guanxin), "reflecting without an object" (wu suo nian), and so on, were, like "bare attention," seen as direct approaches that circumvented the need for traditional dhyāna attainments, for mastery of scripture and doctrine, and for proficiency in monastic ritual. In brief, the early Zen technique (or techniques—it is difficult to determine whether these terms were referring to one and the same practice) revolved around a seemingly simple figure–ground shift, wherein attention is directed away from objects of any kind toward the abiding "luminosity" or "transparency" of mind or awareness itself. The early Zen reformers, like the Burmese reformers in the twentieth century, were popularizers: they touted a method that was simple, promised quick results, and could be cultivated by anyone in a short period of time. Indeed, one early Zen text, attributed to the fourth patriarch Daoxin (580–651), actually traces the technique back to Layman Fu.[24]

Early Zen was not the only premodern Buddhist tradition to develop something akin to "bare attention"; one finds it in Tibetan Dzogchen as well, which is not surprising as there is evidence, albeit controversial, that Dzogchen was itself influenced by Zen.[25] I do not want to engage the thorny issue of whether these traditions were referencing a common meditative experience or state of consciousness.[26] Rather, I would draw attention to certain institutional and sociological parallels—to the fact that the early Zen patriarchs and Dzogchen masters, like their modern Burmese counterparts, were interested in developing a method simple enough to be accessible to those who were unschooled in Buddhist doctrine and scripture, who were not necessarily wedded to classical Indian cosmology, who may not have had the time or inclination for extended monastic practice, and who were interested in immediate results as opposed to incremental advancement over countless lifetimes. It is thus not surprising that the early Zen and Dzogchen teachers found themselves in the same position as Mahāsi: castigated for dumbing down the tradition, for devaluing ethical training, for misconstruing or devaluing the role of wisdom, and for their crassly "instrumental" approach to practice.

Those interested in the scientific, empirical study of mindfulness today would do well to pay attention to some of these criticisms. The Tang master Mazu Daoyi (709–88), for example—a celebrated representative of the Hongzhou Zen lineage—was noted for his rejection of the more scholastic interests of the monks in his day, and he is particularly associated with the idea of a sudden, almost spontaneous, realization of one's buddha nature or "true mind." But Guifeng Zongmi (780–841), another celebrated master and chronicler of early Zen, had deep misgivings. He believed that the Hongzhou method, which he characterizes as "simply giving free rein to the mind" (*dun renxin*), failed to distinguish between right and wrong.[27] Indeed, a not uncommon criticism was that the excessive focus in meditation on achieving "inner stillness" (*ningji*), especially when unbalanced by an engagement with the scriptures, leads to a state described as "falling into emptiness" (*duokong*), which is, in turn, associated with "meditation sickness" (*chanbing*).[28] The term "meditation sickness" was used by various Buddhist masters as a critique of practices they deemed detrimental to the path, notably techniques that emphasized inner stillness—they seem to have been targeting practices that cultivated a sort of noncritical or nonanalytical presentness. Today we might translate "meditation sickness" as "zoning out," by which I do not mean being lost in thought or daydreaming. Rather, I suspect that when medieval meditation masters used terms such as "falling into emptiness" and "meditation sickness," they were targeting techniques that resulted in an intense immersion in the moment, in the now, such that the practitioner loses touch with the socially, culturally, and historically constructed world in which he or she lives. The practitioner becomes estranged from the web of social relations that are the touchstone of our humanity as well as our sanity. The key to avoiding this is to learn to see both sides at once. Zongmi says: "While awakening from delusion is sudden, the transformation of an unenlightened person into an enlightened person is gradual." From a more traditional Buddhist perspective, what is missing in the modern mindfulness movement is precisely this gradual transformation, which involves active engagement with Buddhist doctrine and Buddhist "forms of life" (*Lebensform*).[29]

THE MODERN MINDFULNESS MOVEMENT

This engagement with Buddhist scripture, doctrine, ritual, and institutions is often rejected by modern advocates of mindfulness, who believe they can garner the rewards of Buddhist practice without having to adopt a Buddhist form of life or world view. Indeed, some insist that Buddhist practice does not entail a worldview at all; rather than a process of reconditioning, they claim that Buddhist meditation, properly understood, is a process of deconditioning—of setting aside our culturally constructed notions of reality so as to see things "as they really are." The object, they believe, is to put an end to the ceaseless inner chatter of the mind—to stop thinking. The epistemological and metaphysical commitments behind this are vividly illustrated in Jill Bolte Taylor's popular book (2008) and TED video,[30] both of which are titled "My Stroke of Insight." Taylor, a brain scientist, experienced what she believes is a taste of Buddhist nirvāna as the result of a debilitating stroke that compromised areas of her left hemisphere. She writes:

> As the language centers in my left hemisphere grew increasingly silent and I became detached from the memories of my life, I was comforted by an expanding sense of grace. In this void of higher cognition and details pertaining to my normal life, my consciousness soared into an all-knowingness, a "being at *one*" with the universe.[31]

Taylor holds that if we can just quiet the inner voice in our left brain, we will spontaneously experience the nirvāna that is always present in our right brain.[32]

In short, the rhetoric of "bare attention" is predicated on an often unacknowledged commitment to what scholars of religious mysticism call "perennialism"—the notion that there is a singular, transcultural, transhistorical, and spiritual experience that is common to mystics around the globe.[33] The perennial experience is, in itself, unconstructed: it is free of local cultural, linguistic, or social inflections, although such inflections invariably color any and all descriptions or analyses of such a state. More specifically, the popular understanding of mindfulness seems to be associated with an understanding of perennialism that is sometimes called the "filter theory." The filter theory, vividly illustrated in Taylor's narrative, holds that our normal sensory and discursive processes, rather than opening us to reality, actually serve to filter it out. The Indian master Kamalaśīla (fl. 740–795), in his critique of the Chinese Zen master Heshang Moheyan (d.u.) in a famous eighth-century Tibetan debate, pointed out that there is a particular place for yogis who erroneously believe that the goal of meditation is to put an end to thinking: it is the realm of the "beings without minds," who, after death, will spend five hundred eons as mindless zombies.[34]

Just as there is a set of metaphysical commitments that undergird the modern mindfulness movement, there are also ethical and political commitments. The problem is that, in America at least, these commitments so resemble those of mainstream consumer culture that they go largely unnoticed. Note that, in the early period at least, the Buddhist institution—known as the *saṃgha*—comprised a renunciate community that embodied, quite literally, a critique of mainstream social values and cultural norms. For the *saṃgha*, liberation required "letting go," and letting go did not mean to merely adopt a particular attitude or psychological frame, however important such a frame may be. Rather, it necessitated a radical change in the way one lived; one was required to opt out of family ties and worldly pursuits, and opt in to an alternative, communal, celibate, and highly regulated lifestyle. Modern teachers of mindfulness rarely make such demands of their students; the liberating, or if you will therapeutic, benefits apparently do not require dramatic changes in the way one lives. Rather than enjoining practitioners to renounce carnal and sensual pleasure, mindfulness is touted as a way to more fulfilling sensual experiences. Rather than enjoining practitioners to renounce mainstream American culture, mindfulness is seen as a way to better cope with it. There may be no better exemplar of this ethically dubious and politically reactionary stance than *Tricycle Magazine*, with its advertisements for expensive meditation gear, for Dharmic dating services, Dharmic dentists and accountants, and its implicit authorization of the entrepreneurial and commercial activities of countless dharma centers and self-styled Buddhist masters. The packaging of mindfulness in programs such as Mindfulness-Based Stress Reduction (MBSR) and Mindfulness-Based Cognitive Therapy (MBCT) is arguably a variant on the same theme.

Could it be that this socially conservative ideology is tied to the particular ideological strand in modern Buddhism that I have identified as perennialism? Arguments to similar effect have been made by, among others, Hannah Arendt and Emmanuel Lévinas,[35] but perhaps most relevant is the so-called "Critical Buddhism" (*Hihan Bukkyō*) movement that emerged out of Japanese Sōtō Zen in the 1990s. The leaders (and possibly sole members) of this movement, Hakamaya Noriaki and Matsumoto Shirō, claimed that the ethical failings of Japanese Buddhist schools—notably their complicity in the militarist and nationalist fever that led up to the Pacific War—could be traced, in part, to buddha-nature theory.[36] (The doctrine of inherent buddha nature holds, in brief, that we are all naturally endowed with the awakened state of the buddhas but fail to recognize it.) Their argument, in short, is that the East Asian Buddhist tradition largely abandoned the more analytical and critical dimensions of Indian Mahāyāna, aligning itself instead with buddha-nature doctrine, and that this led to a kind of ethical, social, and political passivity. This is not the place to weigh in on this issue, except to note that this critique too emerges not from without but from within the Buddhist tradition itself.[37]

CONCLUSION

To conclude, it is my impression that many of the psychologists, cognitive scientists, and sociologists doing research on Burmese-style mindfulness practices seem to assume that the psychological benefits of such practice are born out by centuries of Buddhist experience. Such is not the case. To the extent that the modern approach to mindfulness can be found in premodern Asia, it was a minority position that was met with considerable criticism from traditional quarters. The nature of the criticism warrants our attention, as it parallels criticism directed against Mahāsi's technique in modern Southeast Asia. Thus we hear the charge that such practices emphasize momentary states rather than long-term transformation, that they do not yield the benefits that are claimed on their behalf, that they are more Hindu than Buddhist, and that the overriding emphasis on inner stillness, in the absence of critical intellectual engagement with the teachings, can lead to a paralyzing state of self-absorption—what East Asian Buddhists have long identified as "meditation sickness."[38]

To be clear, I am not claiming that mindfulness has no therapeutic value. I am aware of the claims, based on a substantial body of empirical (if contested) data, that suggest it does. But my own experience among long-term meditators in Asian monastic settings as well as in American practice centers leads me to be somewhat skeptical, and I sometimes wonder if researchers in this area are asking the right questions of the right people. It is not just that advanced meditation practitioners in more traditional Asian settings may not exhibit the kinds of behavior that we associate with mental health. It is that, as Obeyesekere noted, it is not clear that they aspire to our model of mental health in the first place. And this, I submit, is the real challenge for those interested in the causal relationship between traditional forms of Buddhist meditation and the psychological and behavioral outcomes that such meditation is assumed to produce.[39]

CODA

*Robert Meikyo Rosenbaum
and Barry Magid*

One of the major insights of Buddhism is that no thing is permanent. As Buddhism becomes more prominent in our society, it is inevitable both Buddhism and our society will change. Hopefully they will remodel each other in ways that preserve the best of both. Surely new forms will develop that we cannot fully envision from our current standpoint.

Whatever forms they take, there is an inherent problem they will need to confront: any practice can become reified. When a practice is taken out of its original context and is codified, instrumentalized, and constrained to become a means to an end, it runs the danger not only of losing many of the rich meanings of its original sources but of getting in the way of what it intends to express. We are reminded of the nineteenth koan in the *Gateless Gate* collection:

JOSHU ASKED NANSEN: "What is the Way?"
NANSEN SAID: "Everyday life is the Way."
JOSHU ASKED: "Can it be studied?"
NANSEN SAID: "If you try to study, you will be far away from it."
JOSHU ASKED: "If I do not study, how can I know it is the Way?"

NANSEN SAID: "The path does not belong to the perception world, neither does it belong to the nonperception world. Cognition is a delusion and noncognition is senseless. If you want to reach the true path beyond doubt, place yourself in the same freedom as sky. You name it neither good nor not-good."

In our introduction, we mentioned that Dogen universally recommended zazen to all people. We asked whether it's possible or even desirable for a practice that was originally an expression of a way of life to be translated into a practical method for achieving particular goals, no matter how laudatory the intent.

Can we form any conclusions? Perhaps it is best to conclude with a quotation from a Zen text, Tozan Ryokai's "Song of the Jewel Mirror Samadhi":

Turning away and touching are both wrong
for it is like a mass of fire.
Just to depict it in literary form
is to relegate it to defilement.

If you're reading this, you are, together with us, engaged in the experiment of integrating meditation—whether it be mindfulness or zazen—into our current society. Whatever we may think about it, this is our practice. Practice is alive—which means it is beyond birth and death, beyond usefulness, beyond gain or loss. *Bodhi Svaha*!

NOTES

INTRODUCTION

1. In his poem "The Point of Zazen, After Zen Master Hongzhi," in Kazuaki Tana-hashi, ed., *Moon in a Dewdrop* (Berkeley: North Point Press, 1985), 219.

2. Case 20 in *Shoyoroku*. Thomas Cleary, trans., *Book of Serenity* (New York: Lindis-farne Press, 1990).

1. MISCHIEF IN THE MARKETPLACE FOR MINDFULNESS

The author thanks the many teachers and practitioners whose conversations have helped him clarify his thoughts on these matters. First and foremost, there is his teacher, Barry Magid. But he also thanks Peter Arcese, Esq.; Hon. Maria Arias; Dr. Jan Chozen Bays; Laren Hogen Bays; Prof. William Blatt; Dr. Ann Burlein; Prof. Deborah Cantrell; Robert Chender, Esq.; Prof. Robin Morris Collin; Prof. Linda Fisher; Angie Gius, JD; Prof. Rachel Godsil; Prof. Victor Goode; Charmaine Henderson, Esq.; Prof. Timothy Iglesias; Prof. Kathryn Judge; Dr. Miriam London; Prof. Rhonda Magee; Prof. Solangel Maldonado; Debra Seido Martin; John McIlwain, Esq.; Evelyn O'Haire; Hugh Tenkan O'Haire; Prof. Stephanie Phillips; Dr. Robert Rosenbaum; Prof. Barbara Schatz; Claire Slemmer; Karen Terzano; Abby Mushin Terris; Sallie Jiko Tisdale; Andrew Tootell; Dr. Larry Juho Trussell; and Nigel Wellings.

1. Caitlin Kelly, "O.K., Google, Take a Deep Breath," *New York Times*, April 29, 2012. Kelly is quoting employee Bill Duane.

2. Kate Murphy, "No Time to Think," *New York Times*, July 25, 2014.

3. Curtis White, "The Science Delusion: An Interview with Cultural Critic Curtis White," *Tricycle*, Spring 2014. White critiques the introduction of deracinated Buddhist practices into industry as not in the interests of workers.

4. See, for example, the following books and organizations: Daniel P. Barbezat and Mirabai Bush, *Contemplative Practices in Higher Education* (San Francisco: Jossey-Bass, 2013). Berkeley Initiative for Mindfulness in Law, http://www.law .berkeley.edu/mindfulness.htm. Center for Contemplative Mind in Society, http:// www.contemplativemind.org/. Melissa Korn and Joe Light, "Business Education: On the Lesson Plan: Feelings—'Soft Skills' Business Courses Aim to Prepare Students for Managerial Roles," *Wall Street Journal*, May 5, 2011. Rhonda V. Magee, "Educating Lawyers to Meditate?" *University of Missouri–Kansas City Law Review* 79 (2011): 535–93. Scott L. Rogers, *Mindfulness for Law Students: Using the Power of Mindful Awareness to Achieve Balance and Success in Law School* (Miami Beach, FL: Mindful Living Press, 2009). Scott L. Rogers, "The Mindful Law School: An Integrative Approach to Transforming Legal Education," *Touro Law Review* 28 (2012): 1189–205. Scott L. Rogers and Jan Jacobowitz, *Mindfulness and Professional Responsibility: A Guide Book for Integrating Mindfulness into the Law School Curriculum* (Miami Beach, FL: Mindful Living Press, 2012). Richard Weiner, "Mindfulness Makes Its Way into Law Schools," *Akron Legal News*, October 17, 2012, http://www.akronlegalnews.com/editorial/5071.

5. The Anxious Lawyer, Mindfulness Training for Lawyers, http://theanxiouslawyer .com/. Georgetown Lawyers in Balance Program, http://www.law.georgetown .edu/campus-life/health-wellness/lawyers-in-balance/index.cfm. Steven Keeva, "Better Than a Massage: Clear Your Mind and Refocus—Right Here, Right Now!" *ABA Journal E-Report* 3, no. 24 (2004): 6. Rogers, *Mindfulness for Law Students*, 2009.

6. Clark Freshman, "After Basic Mindfulness Meditation: External Mindfulness, Emotional Truthfulness, and Lie Detection in Dispute Resolution," *Journal of Dispute Resolution.* (2006): 511–22. See also the following: Clark Freshman, Adele M. Hayes, and Greg C. Feldman, "Adapting Meditation to Promote Negotiation Success: A Guide to Varieties and Scientific Support," *Harvard Negotiation Law Review* 7 (2002): 67–81. Diane Musho Hamilton, *Everything Is Workable: A Zen Approach to Conflict Resolution* (Boston: Shambhala, 2013). Barry Nobel, "Meditation and Mediation," *Family Court Review* 43 (2005): 295. Leonard L. Riskin, "The Contemplative Lawyer: On the Potential Contributions of Mindfulness Meditation to Law Students, Lawyers, and Their Clients," *Harvard Negotiation Law*

Review 7 (2002): 1–66. Leonard L. Riskin, "Mindfulness: Foundational Training for Dispute Resolution," *Journal of Legal Education* 54 (2004): 79–90. Leonard L. Riskin, "Further Beyond Reason: Emotions, the Core Concerns, and Mindfulness in Negotiation," *Nevada Law Journal* 10 (2010): 289–337. Leonard L. Riskin, "Awareness and the Legal Profession: An Introduction to the Mindful Lawyer Symposium," *Journal of Legal Education* 61 (2012): 634–40. WarriorOne, Essential Mindfulness for Lawyers: Smarter, Saner Practice. http://www.warriorone.com/.

7. William S. Blatt, "What's Special About Meditation? Contemplative Practice for American Lawyers," *Harvard Negotiation Law Review* 7 (2002): 125–41. Blatt makes reference to Daniel Goleman, *Emotional Intelligence: Why It Can Matter More than IQ* (New York: Bantam, 1995); and Daniel Goleman, *Working with Emotional Intelligence* (New York: Bantam, 1998).

8. Deborah Calloway, *Becoming a Joyful Lawyer: Contemplative Training in Non-Distraction, Empathy, and Emotional Wisdom* (Self-published, University of Connecticut Law School, 2012). Steven W Keeva, "Practicing from the Inside Out," *Harvard Negotiation Law Review* 7 (2002): 97–107.

9. Nancy Levit and Douglas O. Linder, *The Happy Lawyer: Making a Good Life in the Law* (Oxford: Oxford University Press, 2010).

10. Douglas A. Codiga, "Reflections on the Potential Growth of Mindfulness Meditation in the Law," *Harvard Negotiation Law Review* 76 (2002): 109–24. Angela P. Harris, "Toward Lawyering as Peacemaking: A Seminar on Mindfulness, Morality, and Professional Identity," *Journal of Legal Education* 61 (2012): 647–53. Magee, "Educating Lawyers," Leonard L. Riskin, "Awareness and Ethics in Dispute Resolution and Law: Why Mindfulness Tends to Foster Ethical Behavior," *South Texas Law Review* 50 (2009): 493–503. Deborah J. Cantrell, "Can Compassionate Practice Also Be Good Legal Practice? Answers from the Lives of Buddhist Lawyers," *Rutgers Journal of Law and Religion* 12 (2010): 1–75. This provides an ethnographic study of Buddhist lawyers.

11. Barry Magid, *Ending the Pursuit of Happiness: A Zen Guide* (Boston: Wisdom Publications, 2008).

12. Gretchen Rubin, *The Happiness Project: Or, Why I Spent a Year Trying to Sing in the Morning, Clean My Closets, Fight Right, Read Aristotle, and Generally Have More Fun* (New York: HarperCollins, 2009).

13. Alina Dizik, "Feeling Transcendent in 10 Minutes or Less." *Wall Street Journal*, October 27, 2011.

14. See also Jeremy Safran, "McMindfulness: The Marketing of Well-Being," *Public Seminar*, June 13, 2014, http://www.publicseminar.org/2014/06/mcmindfulness/.

15. Sue McGreevey, "Eight Weeks to a Better Brain: Meditation Study Shows Changes Associated with Awareness, Stress," *Harvard Gazette*, January 21, 2011. Sarah McLean, *Soul-Centered: Transform Your Life in 8 Weeks with Meditation* (Carlsbad, CA: Hay House, 2012). Mark Williams and Danny Penman, *Mindfulness: An Eight Week Plan for Finding Peace in a Frantic World* (New York: Rodale, 2011).

16. Mindfulness Meditation New York Collaborative, http://www.mindfulnessmeditationnyc.com/Homepage. See in particular the Mindfulness Meditation New York Collaborative Mission Statement, http://www.mindfulnessmeditationnyc .com/mission-statement.

17. Kate Pickert, "The Art of Being Mindful," *TIME*, February 3, 2014, 40.

18. For some of these claims, see the following: Rick Hanson and Richard Mendius, *Buddha's Brain* (Oakland, CA: New Harbinger, 2009). Matthieu Ricard, "This Is Your Brain on Mindfulness," in *The Mindfulness Revolution*, ed. Barry Boyce and the editors of *Shambhala Sun* (Boston: Shambhala, 2011), 127–35. Daniel J. Siegel, *The Mindful Brain: Reflection and Attunement in the Cultivation of Well-Being* (New York: W.W. Norton, 2007). Daniel J. Siegel, "Mindfulness Training and Neural Integration: Differentiation of Distinct Streams of Awareness and the Cultivation of Well-Being," *Social Cognitive and Affective Neuroscience* 2, issue 4 (2007): 259.

19. Eihei Dogen, "Rules for Zazen," trans. D. Welch and Kazuaki Tanahashi, in *Moon in a Dewdrop*, ed. Kazuaki Tanahashi (Berkeley: North Point Press, 1985), 30.

20. Kosho Uchiyama, *Opening the Hand of Thought: Approach to Zen*, trans. Shohaku Okumura and Tom Wright, ed. Jisho Cary Warner (New York: Penguin, 1993).

2. "I" DOESN'T MIND

1. Throughout this essay, when quoting koans, I draw on and combine several translations. Here, I use the translations of Thomas Cleary and J. C. Cleary, *The Blue Cliff Record* (Boston: Shambhala, 1992), and Katsuki Sekida, *Two Zen Classics* (New Haven, CT: Weatherhill, 1996).

2. Soma Thera, "The Way of Mindfulness: The Satipatthana Sutta and Its Commentary," *Access to Insight (Legacy Edition)*, November 2013, http://www.accessto insight.org/lib/authors/soma/wayof.html.

3. Case 5 from the Kattoshu. Thomas Kirchner, trans., *Entangling Vines: A Classic Collection of Zen Koans* (Boston: Wisdom Publications, 2013).

4. Joseph Goldstein and Jack Kornfield, *Seeking the Heart of Wisdom* (Boston: Shambhala, 1987), 56–57.

5. This quote is a paraphrase from Tozan Ryokai's *The Song of Jewel Mirror Samadhi*, which is frequently chanted at Zen services.

6. Case 41 from the *Mumonkan*. Robert Aitken, *The Gateless Barrier: The Wu-men Kuan* (San Francisco: North Point Press, 1990), also Sekida, *Two Zen Classics*, 1977 edition.

7. This is a compilation I have assembled from the translations by John Blofeld, *The Zen Teaching of Huang Po* (New York: Grove Press, 1958), and Lok To, *The Dharma of Mind Transmission: Zen Teachings of Huang Po* (https://www .ic.sunysb.edu/Clubs/buddhism/huangbo/main.html#cl). A similar sentiment is expressed in the earlier Xinxinming by Jianzhi Sengcan, which states, "To seek Mind with the (discriminating) mind is the greatest of all mistakes."

8. James Green, *The Recorded Sayings of Zen Master Joshu* (Boston: Shambhala, 2001), 42.

9. In Kazuaki Tanahashi, ed., *Moon in a Dewdrop* (Berkeley: North Point Press, 1985), 72.

10. Jon Kabat-Zinn, *Wherever You Go, There You Are: Mindfulness Meditation in Everyday Life* (New York: Hyperion Books, 1994).

11. Paraphrased from the translations by Aitken and Sekida. See note 6.

12. Dogen, "Uji, The Time Being," in *Moon in a Dewdrop*, ed. Kazuaki Tanahashi (Berkeley: North Point Press, 1985), 77.

13. Written by Dogen c. 1238. "Shobogenzo ikka no myoju: One bright pearl," in N. Waddell and A. Musao, trans., Eastern Buddhist Compendium IV(2), 1971, 108–17.

14. Written by Dogen c. 1249. "An unbeneficial philosophy about soul and spirit," in *Dogen's Extensive Record (Eihei Koroku)*, trans. Taigen Dan Leighton and Shohaku Okumura (Somerville, MA: Wisdom Publications, 2010), 359.

15. Thich Nhat Hanh, *Transformation at the Base: Understanding Our Mind* (Berkeley: Parallax Press, 2001), 137–38.

16. *Tao Te Ching*, verse 64. This version, assembled from several translations, can be found in my book *Walking the Way: 81 Zen Encounters with the Tao Te Ching* (Boston: Wisdom Publications, 2013), 258.

17. *Tao Te Ching*, verse 17. *Walking the Way*, 65.

18. Dogen, "Body-and-Mind Study of the Way (Shinjin Gakudo)," in *Moon in a Dewdrop*, 87–88.

19. Dogen, "Sangai-Yuishin: The Triple World Is Only Mind," in *Shobogenzo, Vol. III*, trans. Gudo Nishijima and Chodo Cross (North Charleston, SC: BookSurge LLC, 1997), 37–42.

20. Dogen comes back to this question again and again. It is central to the Genjo Koan, "Actualizing the Fundamental Point," in *Shobogenzo*, though the quotation

used here is from the Shinjin Gakudo ("Body Mind Study of the Way"), in *Moon in a Dewdrop*, 88.

21. Dogen, "The Reality of Just Sitting," *Dogen's Extensive Record (Eihei Koroku)*, ed. Taigen Dan Leighton (Boston: Wisdom Publications, 2010), 305.

3. THE THREE SHAKY PILLARS OF WESTERN BUDDHISM

Dr. Magid thanks Nigel Wellings, Andrew Tootell, and Prof. Ann Burlein for thoughtful comments on a draft of this chapter.

Professor Poirier thanks the many teachers and practitioners whose conversations have helped him clarify his thoughts on these matters. They include Peter Arcese, Esq.; Hon. Maria Arias; Jan Chozen Bays; Laren Hogen Bays; Prof. William Blatt; Prof. Deborah Cantrell; Robert Chender, Esq.; Prof. Robin Morris Collin; Prof. Linda Fisher; Angie Gius, JD; Prof. Rachel Godsil; Prof. Victor Goode; Charmaine Henderson, Esq.; Prof. Timothy Iglesias; Miriam London; Prof. Rhonda Magee; Prof. Solangel Maldonado; Debra Seido Martin; John McIlwain, Esq.; Evelyn O'Haire; Hugh Tenkan O'Haire; Prof. Stephanie Phillips; Robert Rosenbaum; Claire Slemmer; Karen Terzano; Abby Mushin Terris; Sallie Jiko Tisdale; Larry Juho Trussell; Nigel Wellings; and especially Professor Poirier's teacher, Barry Magid, MD.

1. See generally David L. McMahan, *The Making of Buddhist Modernism* (Oxford: Oxford University Press, 2008); and Jay Michaelson, *Evolving Dharma: Meditation, Buddhism, and the Next Generation of Enlightenment* (Berkeley: North Atlantic Books, 2013).

2. See, e.g., Barry Boyce and the editors of *Shambhala Sun*, eds., *The Mindfulness Revolution* (Boston: Shambhala, 2011), 119–90 (ten excerpts on different aspects of "mindfulness, health, and healing").

3. Philip Kapleau, *The Three Pillars of Zen: Teaching, Practice, and Enlightenment* (New York: Anchor, 1965).

4. Jeremy Safran, "McMindfulness: The Marketing of Well-Being," *Public Seminar*, June 13, 2014, http://www.publicseminar.org/2014/06/mcmindfulness/. Daniel J. Siegel, *Mindsight: The New Science of Personal Transformation* (New York: Bantam, 2011).

5. For example: Jan Chozen Bays, *Mindful Eating: A Guide to Rediscovering a Healthy and Joyful Relationship with Food* (Boston: Shambhala, 2009). Sharon Begley, *Train Your Mind, Change Your Brain: How a New Science Reveals Our Extraordinary Potential to Transform Ourselves* (New York: Ballantine, 2008). Christopher K. Germer, *The Mindful Path to Self-Compassion: Freeing Yourself*

from Destructive Thoughts and Emotions (New York: Guilford Press, 2009). Also see Boyce, *The Mindfulness Revolution*, and Siegel, *Mindsight*.

6. Boyce, *The Mindfulness Revolution*.

7. Pat Enkyo O'Hara, "Which River Will You Cross?" *Buddhadharma*, Fall 2014, 7–8.

8. Buddhist psychotherapist Dr. Miles Neale first coined the term "McMindfulness" during his interview for "Frozen Yoga and McMindfulness: A Critical Perspective on the Mainstreaming of Contemplative Practice," *Shambhala Sun Space*, 2010.

9. Barry Magid, *Nothing Is Hidden: The Psychology of Zen Koans* (Boston: Wisdom Publications, 2013).

10. Dogen, "Genjō Kōan (Actualizing the Fundamental Point)," in *Moon in a Dewdrop: Writings of Zen Master Dōgen, Genjō Kōan*, trans. Robert Aitken and Kazuaki Tanahashi, ed. Kazuaki Tanahashi (Berkeley: North Point Press, 1985), 69–73.

11. See generally Robert Aitken, *The Practice of Perfection: The Pāramitās from a Zen Buddhist Perspective* (New York and San Francisco: Pantheon, 1994).

12. V. Hori, "Buddhist Monasticism in Canada: Sex and Celibacy," in *Flowers on the Rock*, eds. J. Harding, V. Hori, and A. Soucy (Montreal: McGill-Queens University Press, 2014).

13. Dogen, "Fukanzazengi (Recommending Zen to All People)," in *Enlightenment Unfolds: The Essential Teachings of Zen Master Dōgen, Fukanzazengi*, trans. Edward Brown and Kazuaki Tanahashi, ed. Kazuaki Tanahashi (Boston: Shambhala, 1999), 32–34.

14. Dogen prescribes full lotus or half-lotus. We suspect that these postures were familiar to Dogen's audience and, if not necessarily comfortable, certainly were not excruciating, as they are to many Westerners. Had Dogen grown up in a culture where people sat on chairs or kneeled, he presumably would have included other postures that also foster stability, stillness, and a straight but not rigid spine. Such is our method of translating *Fukanzazengi* to our students.

15. Koans, or public cases, often paradoxical or riddle-like, form the core of a different Japanese Zen tradition, Rinzai Zen. Koans appear in Dogen's writings, and we study and use them, but not in a systematized way as a formal curriculum. Other Zen traditions, from Korea, Vietnam, and China, deploy other approaches—bowing, chanting, walking, repeating a phrase in a mantra-like way—as well as sitting and koan study.

16. T. G. Foulk, "Dogen's Use of Rujing's 'Just Sit' (shikan taza) and Other Koans," in *Dogen and Soto Zen*, ed. S. Heine (New York: Oxford, 2015).

17. Charlotte Joko Beck, *Everyday Zen: Love and Work* (New York: HarperOne, 2007). Charlotte Joko Beck and Steve Smith, *Nothing Special* (New York: Harper-One, 1994).

18. See, for example, the following books: H. Aronson, *Buddhist Practice on Western Ground* (Boston, Shambhala, 2013). Mark Epstein, *Thoughts Without a Thinker: Psychotherapy from a Buddhist Perspective*, rev. ed. (New York: Basic Books, 2013). Barry Magid, *Ordinary Mind: Exploring the Common Ground of Zen and Psychiatry* (Boston: Wisdom Publications, 2005) and *Nothing Is Hidden*. Christopher K. Germer, Ronald D. Siegel, and Paul R. Fulton, eds., *Mindfulness and Psychotherapy* (New York and London: Guilford Press, 2005). Diane Eshin Rizzetto, *Waking Up to What You Do: A Zen Practice for Meeting Every Situation with Intelligence and Compassion* (Boston: Shambhala, 2006). Robert Rosenbaum, *Zen and the Heart of Psychotherapy* (Philadelphia: Brunner/Mazel, 1999).

19. R. Sharf, "Is Mindfulness Buddhist? (And Why It Matters)," *Transcultural Psychiatry* 52, no. 4 (2015): 470–84.

20. Enmei Jukku Kannon Gyō, Ordinary Mind Zendō Sutra Book, http://www.ordinarymind.com/sutra-book.

4. MINDFULNESS MYTHS

1. The translation is my own, culled from several sources as described in my book *Walking the Way: 81 Zen Encounters with the Tao Te Ching* (Boston: Wisdom Publications, 2013).

2. As both a psychotherapy researcher and neuropsychologist, I can attest to the difficulties in constructing good assessment measures. Though I describe a few of the problems with ill-conceived outcome measures later in this chapter, the technical issues are immense and beyond the scope of this chapter. Whole volumes are written on the statistical, conceptual, and methodological issues.

3. I've paraphrased the story, which can be found in many places. One source is Christina Feldman and Jack Kornfield, eds., *Stories of the Spirit, Stories of the Heart* (New York: Harper Collins, 1991).

4. M. Sams, R. Aulanko, Hamalainen, et al., "Seeing Speech: Visual Information from Lip Movements Modifies Activity in the Human Auditory Cortex," *Neuroscience Letter* 127 (1991): 141–45.

5. R. Yuste and G. Church, "The New Century of the Brain," *Scientific American*, March 1, 2014, 40.

6. C. R. Harrington, T. C. Beswick, M. Graves, et al., "Activation of the Mesostriatal Reward Pathway with Exposure to Ultraviolet Radiation (UVR) vs. Sham

UVR in Frequent Tanners: A Pilot Study," *Addiction Biology*, April 11, 2011: doi: 10.1111/j.1369-1600.2010.00312.x.

7. S. Martin, "The Power of the Relaxation Response," *Monitor on Psychology* 39, no. 9 (2008): 32.

8. V. Heffernan, "The Muddied Meaning of Mindfulness," *New York Times Magazine*, April 14, 2015.

9. R. Davidson, "Empirical Explorations of Mindfulness: Conceptual and Methodological Conundrums," *Emotion* 10, no. 1 (2010): 8–11.

10. To name just a few: The Freiburg Mindfulness Inventory, the Kentucky Inventory of Mindfulness Skills (KIMS), the Mindful Attention Awareness Scale (MAAS), the Five-Facet Mindfulness Questionnaire, the Cognitive Affective Mindfulness Scale-Revised, the Toronto Mindfulness Scale, the Philadelphia Mindfulness Scale, and the Southampton Mindfulness Questionnaire.

11. Britton, Haynes, Fridel, and Bootzin, "Polysomnographic and Subjective Profiles of Sleep Continuity Before and After Mindfulness-Based Cognitive Therapy in Partially Remitted Depression," *Psychosomatic Medicine* 72 (2010): 539–48.

12. D. S. Black, "Mindfulness-Based Interventions: An Antidote to Suffering in the Context of Substance Abuse, Misuse, and Addiction," *Substance Use and Misuse* 49, no. 5 (2014): 489.

13. B. Khoury, T. Lecomte, G. Fortin, et al., "Mindfulness-Based Therapy: A Comprehensive Meta-Analysis," *Clinical Psychology Review* 33, no. 6 (2013): 763–71.

14. R. A. Baer, "Mindfulness Training as a Clinical Intervention: A Conceptual and Empirical Review," *Clinical Psychology: Science and Practice* 10, no. 2 (2003): 125–43. P. N. L. Grossman, S. Schmidt, H. Walach, "Mindfulness-Based Stress Reduction and Health Benefits: A Meta-Analysis," *Journal of Psychosomatic Research* 57 (2004). E. Bohlmeijer, R. Prenger, E. Taal, P. Cuijpers, "The Effects of Mindfulness-Based Stress Reduction Therapy on Mental Health of Adults with a Chronic Medical Disease: A Meta-Analysis," *Journal of Psychosomatic Research* 68, no. 6 (2010): 539–44. A. Chiesa and A. Serretti, "Mindfulness-Based Stress Reduction for Stress Management in Healthy People: A Review and Meta-Analysis," *The Journal of Alternative and Complementary Medicine* 15, no. 5 (2009): 593–600. S. G. Hofmann, A. T. Sawyer, A. A. Witt, D. Oh, "The Effect of Mindfulness-Based Therapy on Anxiety and Depression: A Meta-Analytic Review," *Journal of Consulting and Clinical Psychology* 78, no. 2: 169–83. D. Ledesma and H. Kumano, "Mindfulness-Based Stress Reduction and Cancer: A Meta-Analysis," *Psycho-Oncology* 18, no. 6 (2009): 571–79.

15. Khoury et al., "Mindfulness-Based Therapy."

16. Database of Abstracts of Reviews of Effects (DARE): Quality-assessed Reviews [Internet], the University of York, Centre for Reviews and Dissemination. http://www.ncbi.nlm.nih.gov/pubmedhealth/PMH0057890/.

17. How effect sizes are calculated, and their meaning, is a complex issue. Basically, the effect size tells how many standard deviations the average person in the experimental (treatment) group is above the average person in the control group. An effect size of .50 is half a standard deviation; an effect size of .20 is one-fifth of a standard deviation. Effect sizes range from 0 to 3, but sizes of around .80 are considered large, .50 moderate, and .20 small.

   If the effect size were 0, a person chosen at random from the experimental group has a 50-50 chance of having a score above a person chosen at random from the control group. In the same scenario of comparing people chosen at random from the two groups, an effect size of .50 gives the participant from the experimental group a 64% chance of being higher, while an effect size of .20 gives a 56% chance. Another way of looking at it is proportion of variance accounted for: an effect size of .50 accounts for around 10% of the variance, while an effect size of .20 accounts for about 1% of the variance between groups.

   By way of comparison, effect sizes of around .50 are common for relaxation training, whereas school-based substance abuse education has an effect size of around .12.

18. S. L. Keng, M. J. Smoski, and C. J. Robins, "Effects of Mindfulness on Psychological Health: A Review of Empirical Studies," *Clinical Psychology Review* 31, no. 6 (2011): 1041–56.

19. M. J. Lambert, "Implications of Outcome Research for Psychotherapy Integration," in *Handbook of Psychotherapy Integration*, eds. J. Norcross and M. Goldstein (New York: Basic Books, 1992), 94–129.

20. B. E. Wampold, *The Great Psychotherapy Debate: Models, Methods, and Findings* (Mahwah, NJ: Lawrence Erlbaum: 2001).

21. For an excellent review of this issue, with a revealing analysis of the research literature, I strongly recommend Art Bohart and Karen Tallman, *How Clients Make Therapy Work: The Process of Active Self-Healing* (Washington, DC: American Psychological Association, 1999).

22. D. Kahneman, *Thinking, Fast and Slow* (New York: Farrar, Straus and Giroux, 2011).

23. The classic "Mirsky model" of attention dates back twenty-five years and has four factors: encode, sustain/stabilize, shift, focus/execute. The model has been revisited in the light of recent findings on large-scale brain systems: see Leonard Koziol, Arthur Joyce, and Glen Wurglitz, "The Neuropsychology of Attention: Revisiting the 'Mirsky Model,' *Applied Neuropsychology: Child* 3 (2014): 297–307.

Another excellent recent article is A. Joyce and S. Hrin, "Attention: An Evolving Construct," *Applied Neuropsychology: Child* 4 (2015): 80–88.

24. P. Wachtel, "Conceptions of Broad and Narrow Attention," *Psychological Bulletin* 68, no. 6 (1967): 417–29.

25. Different schools of Buddhism posit different numbers and kinds of consciousness. One systems posits nine consciousnesses, which, oversimplifying, are the five sense-consciousnesses (seeing, hearing, etc.), a sixth consciousness that integrates the first five, a seventh consciousness that involves formations of abstract thought including a self-concept, an eighth consciousness known as the "storehouse" consciousness, and a ninth, fundamental and pure consciousness.

26. J. Bargh and T. Chartrand, "The Unbearable Automaticity of Being," *American Psychologist* 54, no. 7 (1999): 462–79.

5. ONE BODY, WHOLE LIFE

1. Private Soto Zen Buddhist document given to the author.

2. Thich Nhat Hanh, "Five Mindfulness Trainings," *For a Future to Be Possible* (Berkeley: Parallax, 1993).

3. *Satipatthana Sutta: The Foundations of Mindfulness* (MN 10), translated from the Pali by Nyanasatta Thera. *Access to Insight*, June 14, 2010. www.accesstoinsight .org/tipitaka/mn/mn.010.nysa.html.

4. Eihei Dogen, *Shobogenzo—The Treasure House of the Eye of the True Teaching*, trans. Rev. Hubert Nearman (Mount Shasta: Shasta Abbey, 2007).

5. Thich Nhat Hanh, *The Miracle of Mindfulness* (Boston: Beacon Press, 1975), 14.

6. Robert Thurman, *The Holy Teaching of Vimalakirti* (University Park: Pennsylvania State, 1988), 70.

7. Thich Nhat Hanh, "Mindfulness Must Be Engaged," *Peace Is Every Step* (Berkeley: Parallax, 1992).

8. Elizabeth Stanley and Amishi Jha, "Mind Fitness: Improving Operational Effectiveness and Building Warrior Resilience," October 30, 2009, http://www.army .mil/mobile/article/?p=29549.

9. "The Thousand Year View: An Interview with Jon Kabat-Zinn," *Inquiring Mind* 30, no. 2 (Spring 2014).

10. http://www.huffingtonpost.com/ron-purser/beyond-mcmindfulness_b_3519289 .html.

11. "Vanijja Sutta: Business (Wrong Livelihood)" (AN 5.177), translated from the Pali by Thanissaro Bhikkhu. Access to Insight (Legacy Edition), 3 July 2010, http:// www.accesstoinsight.org/tipitaka/an/an05/an05.177.than.html.

12. Stanley and Jha, "Mind Fitness."

13. Stanley and Jha, "Mind Fitness."

14. Brian Daizen Victoria, *Zen at War* (Summit, PA: Rowman & Littlefield, 2006). See also Brian Daizen Victoria, *Zen War Stories* (London: Routledge, 2003).

15. From *Zen for Americans* by Soyen (sic) Shaku, 1906. http://www.sacred-texts .com/bud/zfa/zfa22.htm.

16. https://www.facebook.com/stephen.batchelor.395/posts/10204978386316098.

6. THE BUFFET

1. Various sources, including Omega's website (http://www.eomega.org/) and Elizabeth Lesser's website (http://www.elizabethlesser.org/), over a number of years.

2. Copy from Omega's website describing the Great Shamanic Initiation class: http://www.eomega.org/workshops/the-great-shamanic-initiation-o?content =ROT&source=OM.home#-workshop-description-block.

7. TWO PRACTICES, ONE PATH

1. Ven. Analayo, trans., *Satipatthana: The Direct Path to Realization* (Cambridge, UK: Windhorse Publications, 2003).

2. Philip Kapleau, *The Three Pillars of Zen: Teaching, Practice, and Enlightenment* (New York: Anchor, 1965).

3. Ariyapariyesana Sutta (MN 1.3). All sutta quotes are from the Middle Length Discourses. All translations from Majjhima Nikaya are by the author.

4. Cula-hatthipadopama Sutta (MN 27:17).

5. Upali Sutta (MN 56:29).

6. Bahuvedaniya Sutta (MN 59:10).

7. Bhaya-bherava Sutta (MN 4:17).

8. Mahatanhasankhaya Sutta (MN 38:30).

9. Kakacupama Sutta (MN 21:7).

10. Pindapataparisuddhi Sutta (MN 151:12).

11. Saccavibhanga Sutta (MN 141:30).

12. Bhaya-bherava Sutta (MN 4).

13. Satipatthana Sutta (MN 10.5).

14. Satipatthana Sutta (MN 10.47).

15. This article, and the dialogue between Gil Fronsdal and Max Erdstein, was originally published in *Inquiring Mind* 31, no. 2 (Spring 2015). © 2015 by *Inquiring Mind*. www.inquiringmind.com. It is reprinted by permission of *Inquiring Mind*.

10. DROWNING IN SUFFERING

1. Jason M. Wirth, ed., *Zen No Sho: The Calligraphy of Fukushima Keido Roshi* (Santa Fe, NM: Clear Light Publishers, 2003), 100. The interview date is given by Wirth on page 3 of his introduction.

EPILOGUE

This research received no specific grant from any funding agency in the public, commercial, or not-for-profit sectors.

1. G. W. Brown and T. O. Harris, *Social Origins of Depression: A Study of Psychiatric Disorder in Women* (New York: Free Press, 1978), 235.

2. G. Obeyesekere, "Depression, Buddhism, and the Work of Culture in Sri Lanka," in *Culture and Depression: Studies in the Anthropology and Cross-Cultural Psychiatry of Affect and Disorder*, ed. A. Kleinman and B. Good (Berkeley: University of California Press, 1985), 134.

3. Buddhaghosa, *The Path of Purification (Visuddhimagga)*, trans. B. Ñāṇamoli, vol. 2 (Berkeley: Shambhala, 1976), 753.

4. For a history of the construal of Buddhism as a "science of happiness," see especially D. S. Lopez, *Buddhism and Science: A Guide for the Perplexed* (Chicago: University of Chicago Press, 2008), and D. S. Lopez, *The Scientific Buddha: His Short and Happy Life* (New Haven, CT: Yale University Press, 2012).

5. The literature on Buddhist modernism is large and growing; see, for example, the collection of papers in D. S. Lopez, ed., *Curators of the Buddha: The Study of Buddhism Under Colonialism* (Chicago: University of Chicago Press, 1995), as well as R. Gombrich and G. Obeyesekere, *Buddhism Transformed: Religious Change in Sri Lanka* (Princeton, NJ: Princeton University Press, 1988); D. L. McMahan, *The Making of Buddhist Modernism* (Oxford: Oxford University Press, 2008); and R. H. Sharf, "Buddhist Modernism and the Rhetoric of Meditative Experience," *Numen* 42, no. 3 (1995): 228–83.

6. The Satipaṭṭhāna Sutta (Majjhima Nikāya 10) and Mahasatipaṭṭhāna Sutta (Dīghānikāya 22); cf. the Chinese Nian chu jing (Taishō shinshū daizōkyō, no. 26, vol. 1, pp. 582b–84c).

7. On Ledi Sayādaw, see especially E. Braun, *The Birth of Insight: Meditation, Modern Buddhism, and the Burmese Monk Ledi Sayadaw* (Chicago: University of Chicago Press, 2013); on Mingun Sayādaw, see G. Houtman, "Beyond the Cradle and Past the Grave: The Biography of Burmese Meditation Master U Ba Khin," in *Sacred Biography in the Buddhist Traditions of South and Southeast Asia*, ed. J. Schober (Honolulu: University of Hawai'i Press, 1997), 311.

8. On Mahāsi's pivotal role in the Burmese lay meditation movement, in addition to Braun, *The Birth of Insight*, see I. Jordt, *Burma's Mass Lay Meditation Movement: Buddhism and the Cultural Construction of Power* (Athens: Ohio University Press, 2007). Braun believes that the lay orientation can be traced back to Ledi who was influenced by, among others, his mentor Hpo Hlaing (1830–85), a layperson working in the Burmese court environment. Hpo Hlaing wrote two popular books on meditation, *Taste of Liberation* (*Vimuttirasa*, 1871) and *Meditation on the Body* (*Kāyanupassanā*, 1874), both of which "reveal a concern for a lay readership and an effort to show meditation's relevance to knowledge about the modern world that presage and likely informed Ledi's presentation of meditation" (Braun, 31). Ledi came to believe that laypersons are capable of advanced stages on the path and that awakening is possible in this very lifetime (Braun, 119), both of which are integral to the ideology of Buddhist modernism. Mahāsi's teacher Mingun is sometimes given credit for establishing the first meditation center in Burma open to laypersons as well as monastics (Houtman, "Beyond the Cradle and Past the Grave," 311).

9. Nyanaponika describes it as follows: "Bare Attention is concerned only with the present. It teaches what so many have forgotten: to live with full awareness in the Here and Now. It teaches us to face the present without trying to escape into thoughts about the past or the future. Past and future are, for average consciousness, not objects of observation, but of reflection. And, in ordinary life, the past and the future are taken but rarely as objects of truly wise reflection, but are mostly just objects of daydreaming and vain imaginings which are the main foes of Right Mindfulness, Right Understanding and Right Action as well. Bare Attention, keeping faithfully to its post of observation, watches calmly and without attachment the unceasing march of time; it waits quietly for the things of the future to appear before its eyes, thus to turn into present objects and to vanish again into the past." Nyanaponika Thera, *The Heart of Buddhist Meditation: A Handbook of Mental Training Based on the Buddha's Way of Mindfulness* (New York: Samuel Weiser, 1973), 40.

10. The secondary literature on the "Mahāsi method" is vast. On the complex doctrinal issues surrounding Mahāsi's method, see especially L. S. Cousins, "The Origins of Insight Meditation," in *The Buddhist Forum IV, Seminar Papers 1994–1996*, ed. T. Skorupski (London: School of Oriental and African Studies, 1996), 35–58. On the influence of the Mahāsi method in contemporary Thai monastic and lay practice, see J. Cook, *Meditation in Modern Buddhism: Renunciation and Change in Thai Monastic Life* (Cambridge, UK: Cambridge University Press, 2010). For its influence in Nepal, see S. LeVine, and D. N. Gellner, *Rebuilding Buddhism:*

The Theravada Movement in Twentieth-Century Nepal (Cambridge, MA: Harvard University Press, 2005).

11. As much has been written of late about the term *sati/smṛti* I will only touch upon it here. In my discussion I am drawing largely on R. Gethin, *The Buddhist Path to Awakening: A Study of the Bodhi-Pakkhiyā Dhammā* (Leiden: E. J. Brill, 1992), 36–44; but see also J. Gyatso, ed., *In the Mirror of Memory: Reflections on Mindfulness and Remembrance in Indian and Tibetan Buddhism* (Albany: SUNY Press, 1992); Tse-fu Kuan, *Mindfulness in Early Buddhism: New Approaches through Psychology and Textual Analysis of Pali, Chinese, and Sanskrit Sources* (London: Routledge, 2008); Nyanaponika, *Abhidhamma Studies: Researches in Buddhist Psychology*, 3rd ed. (Kandy, Sri Lanka: Buddhist Publication Society, 1976), 68–72; E. Shulman, "Mindful Wisdom: The *Sati-Paṭṭhāna-Sutta* on Mindfulness, Memory, and Liberation," in *History of Religions* 49, no. 4: 393–42; and the special 2011 issue of *Contemporary Buddhism* on the topic "Mindfulness: Diverse perspectives on its meaning, origins, and multiple applications at the intersection of science and dharma" (vol. 12, no. 1).

12. Samyutta Nikāya, vol. 5, 197–98; trans. Gethin, in *The Buddhist Path to Awakening*, 36.

13. "Just as, Your Majesty, the treasurer of a king who is a *cakka-vattin* causes the *cakka-vattin* king to remember his glory evening and morning [saying], 'So many, lord, are your elephants, so many your horses, so many your chariots, so many your foot soldiers, so much your gold, so much your wealth, so much your property; may my lord remember.' Thus he calls to mind the king's property. Even so, your Majesty, *sati*, when it arises, calls to mind *dhammas* that are skillful and unskillful, with faults and faultless, inferior and refined, dark and pure, together with their counterparts: these are the four establishings of mindfulness, these are the four right endeavors, these are the four bases of success, these are the five faculties, these are the five powers, these are the seven awakening-factors, this is the noble eight-factored path, this is calm, this is insight, this is knowledge, this is freedom." *Milindapañha* 37; trans. Gethin, in *The Buddhist Path to Awakening*, 37.

14. "By means of it they [i.e., other *dhammas*] remember, or it itself remembers, or it is simply just remembering, thus it is sati. Its characteristic is not floating; its property is not losing; its manifestation is guarding or the state of being face to face with an object; its basis is strong noting or the *satipaṭṭhānas* of the body and so on. It should be seen as like a post due to its state of being firmly set in the object, and as like a gatekeeper because it guards the gate of the eye and so on." *Visuddhimagga* XIV, 141; trans. Gethin, in *The Buddhist Path to Awakening*, 40.

15. Gethin, *The Buddhist Path to Awakening*, 39.

16. On the relationship between *smṛti* and memory and *smṛti* as mindfulness, see especially C. Cox, "Mindfulness and Memory: The Scope of *Smṛti* from Early Buddhism to the Sarvāstivādin Abhidharma," in *In the Mirror of Memory: Reflections on Mindfulness and Remembrance in Indian and Tibetan Buddhism*, ed. J. Gyatso (New York: SUNY Press, 1992), 67–108.

17. See, for example, the analysis in F. Deleanu, *Mind Only and Beyond: An Introduction for the Formation and Early History of the Path of Spiritual Cultivation in Yogācāra Buddhism* (Unpublished manuscript, n.d); and A. C. Klein and T. Wangyal, *Unbounded Wholeness: Dzogchen, Bon, and the Logic of the Nonconceptual* (Oxford: Oxford University Press, 2006). The notion of a nonconceptual state of consciousness was the subject of considerable discussion if not controversy, as it was not easy to square with earlier systems of Buddhist thought. One problem was how to disambiguate states of "nonconceptualization" from states in which there is simply no cognition whatsoever, such as *nirodha-samāpatti* (and, perhaps, *nirvāna*); see R. H. Sharf, "Is Nirvāna the Same as Insentience? Chinese Struggles with an Indian Buddhist Ideal," in *India in the Chinese Imagination: Myth, Religion, and Thought*, eds. J. Kieschnick and Meir Shahar (Philadelphia: University of Pennsylvania Press, 2014), 141–70.

18. Interestingly, some recent findings in cognitive neuroscience resonate with classical Buddhist "intentional" models; see F. J. Varela, E. Thompson, and E. Rosch, *The Embodied Mind: Cognitive Science and Human Experience* (Cambridge, MA: MIT Press, 1991).

19. The only candidate in early Buddhist psychology for a "raw feel" might be *sparśa* or "contact" (Pali: *phassa*), but properly speaking *sparśa* per se is not a conscious event so much as an essential but subliminal constituent involved in the arising of cognition.

20. P. J. Griffiths, *On Being Mindless: Buddhist Meditation and the Mind-Body Problem* (La Salle, IL: Open Court, 1986); P. J. Griffiths, "Pure Consciousness and Indian Buddhism," in *The Problem of Pure Consciousness: Mysticism and Philosophy*, ed. R. K. C. Forman (Oxford: Oxford University Press, 1990), 71–97; Sharf, "Is Nirvāna the Same as Insentience?"

21. R. H. Sharf, "Experience" in *Critical Terms for Religious Studies*, ed. M. C. Taylor (Chicago: University of Chicago Press, 1998), 94–116.

22. For traditionalist critiques see the overview and bibliography in Sharf, *Buddhist Modernism and the Rhetoric of Meditative Experience*, 262–65. The appropriateness of "bare attention" as a way to understand sati is the subject of a dialogue between Alan Wallace and Bhikkhu Bodhi, *The Nature of Mindfulness and Its Role in Buddhist Meditation: A Correspondence Between B. Alan Wallace and the Venerable Bhikkhu Bodhi* (Unpublished manuscript, Santa Barbara Institute for

Consciousness Studies, Santa Barbara, CA, 2006), and is explored at length in several of the contributions to the 2011 issue of *Contemporary Buddhism* (see note 11 above).

23. R. H. Sharf, "Mindfulness and Mindlessness in Early Chan," *Philosophy East & West: A Quarterly of Comparative Philosophy* 64, no. 4 (2014): 933–64.

24. On Layman Fu, or Fu Xi (a.k.a. Fu Dashi, 497–569), see B. H. Hsiao, *Two Images of Maitreya: Fu Hsi and Pu-tai Ho-shang* (Unpublished doctoral dissertation, SOAS, University of London, 1995), 50–224; S. Yanagida, *Shoki no zenshi I* (Kyoto, Japan: Chikuma shobō, 1971), 236; and Y. Zhang, *Fu dashi yanjiu* (Chengdu, PRC: Bashu shushe, 2000). A text attributed to him, the *Shanhui Daishi lu* (*Zokuzōkyō* 69, no. 1335) contains little with regard to actual meditation technique.

25. The Dzogchen analogue to bare awareness is known variously as "awareness" (*rig pa*, sometimes translated "open awareness"), "gnosis" (*ye shes*), "the mind of awakening" (*byang chub kyi sems*), "luminosity" (*'od gsal*, sometimes translated "clear light"), and so on; see S. G. Karmay, *The Great Perfection* (rDzogs Chen): *A Philosophical and Meditative Teaching of Tibetan Buddhism* (Leiden: E. J. Brill, 2007); Klein and Wangyal, *Unbounded Wholeness: Dzogchen, Bon, and the Logic of the Nonconceptual*; and S. van Schaik, *Approaching the Great Perfection: Simultaneous and Gradual Approaches to Dzogchen Practice in Jigme Lingpa's Longchen Nyingtig* (Boston: Wisdom Publications, 2003).

26. Elsewhere I have argued that to do so would be to misconstrue the logic of the rhetoric of "subjective experience" (Sharf, "Experience").

27. For Zongmi's critique of Mazu and the Hongzhou school see J. L. Broughton, *Zongmi on Chan* (New York: Columbia University Press, 2009), 84–86, and passim.

28. This language of inner stillness and falling into emptiness is found, among other places, in the records of another Hongzhou school critic Fayan Wenyi (885–958) and his dharma brother Xiufu (d. 951?). Wenyi's Fayan lineage stressed the study of doctrine and texts as a corrective; see his biography in fascicle 24 of the *Jingde chuangdeng lu* (*Taishō shinshū daizōkyō* no. 2076, vol. 51, 400b1–3), and the discussion in A. Welter, *The Linji Lu and the Creation of Chan Orthodoxy: The Development of Chan's Records of Sayings Literature* (Oxford: Oxford University Press, 2008), 32–33; and B. Brose, *Buddhist Empires: Patronage, Lineage, and the Rise of Chan in China* (Unpublished manuscript, 2013), 116. Guishan Lingyou (771–853), a third-generation teacher in the Hongzhou line, was another critic of a perceived tendency toward moral turpitude in the growing Zen movement; see T. Kirchner, "The Admonitions of Zen Master Guishan Dayuan," *Hanazono daigaku kokusai zengaku kenkyūjo ronshū* 1 (2006): 1–18; and M. Poceski, "Guishan jingce (Guishan's Admonitions) and the Ethical Foundations of Chan Practice," in *Zen Classics: Formative Texts in the History of Zen Buddhism*, eds. S. Heine and D.

S. Wright (Oxford: Oxford University Press, 2006), 15–42. On meditation illness see J. Ahn, *Malady of Meditation: A Prolegomenon to the Study of Illness and Zen* (Unpublished doctoral dissertation, Berkeley: University of California, 2007).

29. P. N. Gregory, "Sudden Enlightenment Followed by Gradual Cultivation," in *Sudden and Gradual: Approaches to Enlightenment in Chinese Thought*, ed. P. N. Gregory (Honolulu: University of Hawai'i Press, 1987), 286. Similar critiques can be found in the writings of many major medieval Zen figures, from Heze Shenhui (670–762?), who played a role in the composition of the Platform Scripture, to Yongming Yanshou (904–975), a prolific and influential master of the tenth century.

30. See http://www.ted.com/talks/jill_bolte_taylor_s_powerful_stroke_of_insight.html.

31. J. B. Taylor, *My Stroke of Insight: A Brain Scientist's Personal Journey* (New York: Viking, 2008), 41.

32. Ibid., 116.

33. The literature on perennialism is vast; for overviews, see especially S. T. Katz, ed., *Mysticism and Philosophical Analysis* (Oxford: Oxford University Press, 1978); S. T. Katz, ed., *Mysticism and Religious Traditions* (Oxford: Oxford University Press, 1983); S. T. Katz, ed., *Mysticism and Language* (Oxford: Oxford University Press, 1992); R. K. C. Forman, ed., *The Problem of Pure Consciousness: Mysticism and Philosophy* (Oxford: Oxford University Press, 1990); W. Proudfoot, *Religious Experience* (Berkeley: University of California Press, 1985); and Sharf, "Experience."

34. Sharf, "Is Nirvāna the Same as Insentience?"

35. R. H. Sharf, "Whose Zen? Zen Nationalism Revisited," in *Rude Awakenings: Zen, the Kyoto School, and the Question of Nationalism*, eds. J. W. Heisig and J. Maraldo (Honolulu: University of Hawai'i Press, 1995), 50–51.

36. J. Hubbard and P. L. Swanson, eds., *Pruning the Bodhi Tree: The Storm Over Critical Buddhism* (Honolulu: University of Hawai'i Press, 1997).

37. On Critical Buddhism, see especially the collection of papers in Hubbard and Swanson, *Pruning the Bodhi Tree*.

38. Ahn, *Malady of Meditation*.

39. This paper was originally prepared for the Advanced Study Institute "Mindfulness in Cultural Context," organized by the Division of Social and Transcultural Psychiatry, McGill University, June 3–5, 2013. A revised version was presented at Smith College on April 4, 2014. My thanks to the audiences at both venues for their comments and critiques. Thanks also to the anonymous reviewers of this paper, whose suggestions, as they will surely note, I did not always follow. And thanks finally to Elizabeth Horton Sharf for her invaluable editorial assistance. Parts of this paper, notably the discussion of the term *smṛti*, borrow directly from my article "Mindfulness and Mindlessness in Early Chan," in *Philosophy East & West*.

INDEX

Page numbers followed by "(2)" indicate two discussions. Page numbers followed by "q" or "+q" indicate quotations or discussions plus quotations.

ABOUT THE CONTRIBUTORS

JANET JIRYU ABELS is the founder and now coresident teacher, with Gregory Hosho Abels, of Still Mind Zendo in New York City (still mindzendo.org) and the guiding teacher of Plum Blossom Zendo in Pittsburgh. She received Dharma transmission as a Zen teacher in the Soto White Plum lineage of Taizan Maezumi Roshi in 2000. She is a certified Bio-Spiritual Focusing teacher and is a member of the White Plum Asanga as well as the Lay Zen Teachers Association. She's the author of *Making Zen Your Own: Giving Life to Twelve Key Golden Age Ancestors.*

MAX ERDSTEIN teaches vipassana meditation at the Insight Meditation Center in Redwood City, California, and the Insight Retreat Center in Santa Cruz. He was trained as a dharma teacher by Gil Fronsdal and participated in the Spirit Rock/IMS teacher training program. He has practiced Vipassana and Zen in California, Japan, Thailand, and Burma. He received lay ordination in the Soto Zen tradition from Sojun Mel Weitsman in 2007.

ZOKETSU NORMAN FISCHER is a poet, writer, and Zen priest. He is the founder and teacher of the Everyday Zen Foundation, a network of Zen (and other) groups and partnerships dedicated to sharing the Zen teaching and practice widely in the world (everydayzen.org). He writes regularly for the Buddhist magazines, and his podcasts are favorites for practitioners from all lineages. The latest of his more than twenty books of poetry, prose, and translation are *Magnolias All At Once* (poetry), *Experience: On Thinking, Writing, Language, and Religion* (essays), and *What Is Zen: Plain Talk for a Beginner's Mind* (prose—written with Sue Moon).

GIL FRONSDAL is part of the Vipassana teachers' collective at Spirit Rock Meditation Center. He was ordained as a Soto Zen priest at the San Francisco Zen Center in 1982 and was a Theravada monk in Burma in 1985. In 1995, he received Dharma transmission from Mel Weitsman, the abbot of the Berkeley Zen Center. He is the guiding teacher of the Insight Meditation Center of Redwood City, California. He has a PhD in Buddhist studies from Stanford University.

MARC R. POIRIER (1952–2015) was a professor of law and Martha Traylor Research Scholar at Seton Hall Law Schools specializing in LGBT and environmental issues. He taught meditation to the students and faculty of his law school and to lawyers and college students in New Jersey and New York City. A longtime practitioner at Ordinary Mind Zendo, he received lay entrustment from his teacher, Barry Magid, and was active in the Lay Zen Teachers Association.

Marc died of lymphoma before this volume could be published. We miss him greatly.

GRACE SCHIRESON is a Dharma teacher in the Suzuki Roshi lineage empowered by Sojun Mel Weitsman, abbot of Berkeley Zen Center. She was asked by Keido Fukushima Roshi, chief abbot of Tofukuji Monastery in Kyoto, Japan, to teach the koans she had studied with him. Grace is the head teacher of the Central Valley Zen Foundation and founded two Zen groups and a Zen retreat center in California. Grace is also a clinical psychologist who has specialized in women and families. She's the author of *Zen Women: Beyond Tea Ladies, Iron Maidens, and Macho Masters.*

HOZAN ALAN SENAUKE is a Zen priest and vice-abbot of Berkeley Zen Center in California. As a Buddhist activist Alan works with the International Network of Engaged Buddhists and the Buddhist Peace Fellowship. He is on the core faculty of Upaya Zen Center's chaplaincy training program. In 2007 he founded Clear View Project, developing Buddhist-based resources for social change in Asia and the US. Alan presently serves as president of the Soto Zen Buddhist Association, a US body of Soto Zen priests. In other lives Alan is a student of American "traditional" music and author of *The Bodhisattva's Embrace: Dispatches from Engaged Buddhism's Front Lines* and *Heirs to Ambedkar: The Rebirth of Engaged Buddhism in India*.

ROBERT H. SHARF is D. H. Chen Distinguished Professor of Buddhist Studies in the Department of East Asian Languages and Cultures, as well as Chair of the Center for Buddhist Studies, at the University of California, Berkeley. He works primarily on medieval Chinese Buddhism but has also published in the areas of Japanese Buddhism, Buddhist art, ritual studies, and methodological issues in the study of religion. In addition to various articles and book chapters, he is the author of *Coming to Terms with Chinese Buddhism: A Reading of the Treasure Store Treatise* (2002), and co-editor of *Living Images: Japanese Buddhist Icons in Context* (2001).

SALLIE JIKO TISDALE is a lay Dharma teacher at Dharma Rain in Portland, Oregon. Her many essays have appeared in *Harper's*, *Antioch Review*, *Conjunctions*, *Threepenny Review*, *The New Yorker*, and *Tricycle*, among other journals. She is the author of seven books, including *Women of the Way*. Her new book, *Violation*, a collection of essays, will be published in 2016 by Hawthorne Books.

SOJUN MEL WEITSMAN established Berkeley Zen Center in Berkeley, California, in 1967 at the behest of his teacher, Shunryu Suzuki. He continues to serve as the abbot and guiding teacher there. He received Dharma transmission in 1984 from Suzuki's son Hoitsu. He is also a former coabbot of the San Francisco Zen Center, where he served from 1988 to 1997.

ABOUT THE EDITORS

 **ROBERT MEIKYO ROSENBAUM** is a neuropsychologist and psychotherapist who now devotes himself full time to Zen and Dayan (Wild Goose) Qigong. He received lay entrustment from Sojun Mel Weitsman of Berkeley Zen Center and is authorized by Master Hui Liu as a senior teacher of the Taoist practice of qigong in the lineage of Yang Meijun. Bob is the founding teacher of the Meadowmont Sangha in the Sierra foothills and the author of *Walking the Way: 81 Zen Encounters with the Tao Te Ching* and *Zen and the Heart of Psychotherapy*. He also enjoys leading annual meditation/qigong trekking retreats in the Nepal Himalayas (zenqigong.com).

 **BARRY MAGID** is a psychiatrist and psychoanalyst practicing in New York City, and the founding teacher of the Ordinary Mind Zendo, also in New York. He is the author of the Wisdom titles *Ordinary Mind: Exploring the Common Ground of Zen and Psychoanalysis*, *Ending the Pursuit of Happiness: A Zen Guide*, and *Nothing Is Hidden: The Psychology of Zen Koans*.

WHAT TO READ NEXT

Mindfulness in Plain English
Bhante Gunaratana

Zen Meditation in Plain English
John Daishin Buksbazen
Foreword by Peter Matthiessen

A New Buddhist Path
Enlightenment, Evolution, and Ethics in the Modern World
David R. Loy

On Zen Practice
Body, Breath, and Mind
Taizan Maezumi and Bernie Glassman
Foreword by Robert Aitken

ALSO AVAILABLE FROM OUR CONTRIBUTORS

Ending the Pursuit of Happiness
A Zen Guide
Barry Magid

Walking the Way
81 Zen Encounters with the Tao Te Ching
Robert Rosenbaum
Foreword by Sojun Mel Weitsman

Making Zen Your Own
Giving Life to Twelve Key Golden Age Ancestors
Janet Jiryu Abels

Zen Women
Beyond Tea Ladies, Iron Maidens, and Macho Masters
Grace Schireson
Foreword by Miriam Levering

About Wisdom Publications

Wisdom Publications is the leading publisher of classic and contemporary Buddhist books and practical works on mindfulness. To learn more about us or to explore our other books, please visit our website at wisdompubs.org or contact us at the address below.

Wisdom Publications
199 Elm Street
Somerville, MA 02144 USA

We are a 501(c)(3) organization, and donations in support of our mission are tax deductible.

Wisdom Publications is affiliated with the Foundation for the Preservation of the Mahayana Tradition (FPMT).